# DO AND TELL:
## Engagement Evangelism in the '70s

D1018341

*by*

GABRIEL FACKRE

WILLIAM B. EERDMANS PUBLISHING COMPANY
GRAND RAPIDS, MICHIGAN

The chapter "A Catechism for Skye" was originally published in *Youth* (July 1972), an ecumenical magazine for young people. Copyright © 1972 United Church Press.

The chapter "Going East: Neomysticism and Christian Faith" is reprinted, by permission, from the April 14, 1971, issue of *The Christian Century*. Copyright 1971 Christian Century Foundation.

*To*
*Mary Comstock Fackre*
*who first told me the Story*

# Acknowledgments

I am grateful to those journals that have allowed me to use previously published material. An earlier Version of "Rethinking Mission" was printed in *Action-Reaction*, edited by Robert Lee and published by San Francisco Theological Seminary. Chapter 2 is part of "A Catechism for Today's Storytellers," a centerfold, with illustrations and supporting material done by my family, in *Youth*, an ecumenical magazine for high school young people edited by Herman C. Ahrens, Jr., and published by the United Church Press in its July 1972 (Vol. XXIII, No. 7) issue. "Going East: Neomysticism and Christian Faith" appeared in *The Christian Century*, Vol. LXXXVIII, No. 15 (April 14, 1971). Thanks go also to Dolores Kronberg, faculty secretary at Andover Newton Theological School, who did her usual able job in typing and retyping my manuscript scrawl.

# Contents

# Introduction

In the fall of 1970 The Church of the Crossroads in Honolulu "gave sanctuary" to a group of young devotees of Hare Krishna. Exuberant mantras and aggressive proselytizing had won the Krishnites the enmity of landlords and neighbors, and they had no place to go. The group had transformed the church school assembly room on Sunday nights into a meditation center complete with lush greenery, candles, mats, and incense. As I sat on the floor among the worshippers engaged in their chanting, dancing, "psychic sleep," and love feast, I wondered where the churches had failed. Almost all of the youthful converts to Krishna have been at least nominal Christians. Had we neglected to get our message across? Or simply proved too hypocritical in the practice of what we preached? Perhaps the only thing left for us to do now was what The Church of the Crossroads had chosen: show its love for the outcaste by being a house of hospitality. Or is there more?

There is more. There is a Tale to be told. We

9

have not been very good at that in recent years.
And the vacuum has something to do with the
exodus of many sensitive spirits. Perhaps that is
understandable. The appeals to bind the wounds
of war, poverty, and race have been urgent. The
church has stumbled out on those roads trying
to respond to these mandates. While doing that,
it almost seemed subversive to give any attention
to things like Tale-telling. But the fact remains
that the Gospel is Good News, word as well as
deed.

Some people are reminding us of this now.
Peter Berger sends out a "call for authority in
the Christian community." Dean Kelley argues
that mainstream churches are declining because
they have neglected their "meaning" ministry.
Lowell Streiker and Gerald Strober talk of a
middle America hungry for a definitive word.
Roger Shinn, while maintaining his commitments to "political theology," urges a more
meaningful partnership between it and personal
and evangelical ministrations.[1] A nationwide
effort in evangelism, Key '73, emerges with
plans to address itself to these matters. And even

---

[1] Peter Berger, "A Call for Authority in the Christian Community," *The Christian Century*, Vol. LXXXVIII, No. 43 (Oct.
27, 1971), pp. 1257-1263; Dean Kelley, *Why the Conservative
Churches Are Growing* (New York: Abingdon, 1972); Lowell D.
Streiker and Gerald Strober, *Religion and the New Majority*
(New York: Association, 1972); Roger Shinn, "Political Theology in Crossfire," *Journal of Current Social Issues*, Vol. X, No.
2 (Spring 1972), pp. 10-20.

denominations that decline to participate in the latter launch their own programs.[2]

For one who has always believed that nurture and sharing the faith had to go on in the midst of our involvement with the social struggle, the recovery is a welcome one. However, there is a new feeling about this dimension of mission. In the setting of the secular-conscious '60s, talk of faith was bashful. Bonhoeffer's "hidden discipline" seemed right, and the place for the display of the pearls of faith appeared to be more the catacombs and less the marketplace. While it is not likely that we have reached the time Bonhoeffer looked for from his prison cell— "that day will come when men will be called again to utter the word of God with such power as will change and renew the world"[3]—it is becoming increasingly clear that the hidden mysteries have to be much more boldly exposed. Our hypnotism with the secular has kept the treasures buried too long. Those prospecting about in cult and occult are trying to tell us something.

We stress here particularly the kind of Talebearing aimed out toward the world—evangelism. Chapter 1 sets the stage for an effort to recover it. Chapter 6 relates it to Krishna-

---

[2] For example, the Deering Conference on Evangelism of the United Church of Christ, July 1972, and the series of articles in *Presbyterian Life*, 1971-1972, on the theme of evangelism.

[3] Dietrich Bonhoeffer, *Prisoner for God: Letters and Papers from Prison*, ed. Eberhard Bethge, trans. Reginald Fuller (New York: Macmillan, 1961), p. 140.

consciousness and other current religious fevers. But evangelism is itself part of a larger mandate, the stewardship of the *kerygma*, or what we shall refer to regularly as "Story-telling." Chapter 2 attempts to say what the Story is, using a modern catechetical method to recount it. Throughout the book we are seeking to unfold the drama and ask how it can be shared with people both inside and outside the church.

But the approach here to proclamation is different. Too many of those eager to get the message across today are making the old mistake of giving the world just what it wants. Not so long ago society announced that it was secular and demanded "relevance." So we gave it a secular theology and a relevant church. Now that "religion" is in, the pious among us feel their moment has come, and the air is filled with "God-talk." We do not want to "worship at these golden calves," as Peter Berger has put it. The Gospel is bigger than the half-truths seized upon to exploit the fads and frenzies of the hour. Right now when the temptation is so strong to reduce the Christian faith to pious phrases and feelings, we need to stand fast for its commitment to earthy action. Religious talk is cheap. What makes the Gospel more than words is its embodiment. "The Word became flesh. . . ." That is a major theme here: telling comes alive in the context of doing. We focus on it especially in Chapters 3, 4, and 5.

A further expression of the refusal to capitulate to the times, even while we seek to relate to them, is to be found in the effort to bring the less visible themes of faith and church into creative tension with the more claimant ones. For example: Christian worship and life together. The last month's writing of the present book went on at the ecumenical research center of St. John's Abbey, Minnesota, where the common life and liturgical rhythm of a Benedictine community drove home the importance of this partnership: "being" and "celebrating" with telling and doing. We reach for that kind of wholeness in the first and last chapters.

If we are really going to get the Word out today, it has to be clear enough to be understood. The "Catechism for Skye" (Ch. 2) is a telling done originally for the ears of youth. Other chapters try to stay in touch with current language and concerns too, but also have footnote-trails off into the less familiar woods of contemporary scholarship. The theological vocation of the writer prompts these sorties, but more, he believes that informed readers will want to get acquainted with some of the wide-ranging discussion of mission. The material, however, has been cleansed of a lot of its jargon by "field-testing" among thousands of laity and clergy at recent church assemblies and evangelism workshops in Ohio, Florida, New Hampshire, Massachusetts, New Jersey, and South

Dakota. It has received its most rigorous scrutiny from my family, who helped me put together the Catechism, and especially from my wife.

Together with clarity, we strive here for objectivity. That seems like a strange note to strike considering the reign these days of subjectivity, the intense absorption with feelings, the interior life, and personal matters. But that is just the point. We have been overwhelmed in the past few years with things visceral and intimate. They have indeed served as a corrective to the unfeeling abstractions that too long passed for theology, and the tendencies toward total preoccupation with corporate and structural issues generated by an era of social ferment. In religion they taught us to remember that truth comes home only when it is "true for me." But now, in some quarters, these accents are in turn becoming imperialistic, inviting mindlessness and escapism. One instance is an evangelism that wallows so extensively in *my* feelings, *my* decision, and *my* salvation that attention is drawn to things that happen to me rather than the divine happenings. Story-telling is, first and foremost, the biography of God, not my autobiography. It is an account of what "he" has done, is doing, and will do. Only in a modest and derivative sense is it concern about our appropriation of these gracious actions. The kind of evangelism we deal with in this book is concerned mainly with what transpires "out there" in the heart and deed of

God, and how that News can best be reported. When that Tale is witnessed to forthrightly, in speech and action, God does the rest; the Word does not return barren.

The decade is full of fresh challenges. One of them is to learn a new love—to love to *do and tell* the Story.

## CHAPTER ONE

# Rethinking Mission

Four decades ago the philosopher and churchman, Ernest Hocking, edited a landmark book, *Rethinking Missions.* New developments within and without the church now again suggest that it is important to reexamine our direction.

Rethinking of purpose and refocus of institutional energies go on all the time, of course. But there are special moments for it. The postwar period was one such occasion, and the rise of liberation movements in the last decade was another. We appear to be on the threshold of yet another as we enter the 1970s.[1] To discern the signs of these new times, it is worth exploring the shape of the past several epochs and the church's response to them.

[1] John Biersdorf has noted the shifting conceptions of ministry that correspond roughly to understandings of mission in "The Crisis in the Ministry," IDOC, North America (New York, 1971), pp. 2-54.

## The Postwar Period and Church-Oriented Mission

The reconstruction years following the Second World War were mobile and rootless, producing a "lonely crowd" on a "quest for community" (book titles frequently reflect the premises of an age).[2] The period was also marked by growing economic security, at least for the middle and upper classes, many of whom were employed by large corporations—an "affluent society" topped by "the organization man."[3] The prospect of atomic cataclysm and the reality of continuing brush-fire wars encouraged speculation about a precarious future and "the causes of World War III."[4] Borrowing ideas from European existentialism, American social analysts and prophets spoke of harried and alienated mass men, cogs in the machine, meaninglessness, apathy, depersonalization, and despair.

Response in the church went on at many levels. Mobile America was followed out to the suburbs by an ecclesiastical building boom. Denominational mission tended to be seen as church extension projects in new areas.[5] Mean-

---

[2] David Riesman with Nathan Glazer and Ruel Denney, *The Lonely Crowd* (Garden City, N. Y.: Doubleday, 1956), and Robert Nisbet, *The Quest for Community* (New York: Oxford U.P., 1953).

[3] John Kenneth Galbraith, *The Affluent Society* (Boston: Houghton Mifflin, 1958), and William H. Whyte, Jr., *The Organization Man* (Garden City, N. Y.: Doubleday, 1956).

[4] C. Wright Mills, *The Causes of World War Three* (New York: Ballantine, 1958, 1960).

[5] Truman Douglass, *Mission to America* (New York: Friendship, 1951).

while, distraught America was addressed with
messages of healing. From the pop deliverances
of Joshua Liebman's *Peace of Mind*, Fulton
Sheen's *Peace of Soul*, Billy Graham's *Peace
with God*, and Norman Vincent Peale's *The
Power of Positive Thinking*, to more sophisticated guides to psychological health such as Til-
lich's *Courage to Be* and Thomas Merton's *Seven
Storey Mountain*, a ministry of personal integra-
tion and wholeness was offered and sought out.

Rising church membership and attendance
figures seemed to vindicate this tack. The
churching of suburbia and the response to the
interpretation of religion as an oasis from the
storm found an audience. The church was seen
as a place of "fellowship" and "peace" that gave
John and Jane Doe back their face and their
name. The clergyman came to be viewed as both
an organizer of this caring community and its
activities, and a pastor whose visits and counseling further embodied the climate of together-
ness. An ecumenical theology that stressed the
church as the Body of Christ further accented
the importance of religious institutions. Will
Herberg could even make a case for his thesis
that religious affiliation, not the ethnic background of former days, gave the typical American his sense of identity and stability.[6]

The church in this era wrote on its banners,
"Come unto me, all you who are weary and

[6] Will Herberg, *Protestant, Catholic, Jew* (New York:
Doubleday, 1956).

heavy laden, and I will give you rest." Mission in
such a time was church-oriented, the act of
drawing people into the beloved community
where they could find themselves. The congregation was a "come structure."

## The Freedom Revolutions and World-Oriented Mission

The 1954 Supreme Court decision to desegre-
gate the public schools heralded a new cultural
development. It took shape in such succeeding
events as the Montgomery bus boycotts, the
freedom rides, the lunch counter sit-ins, the
voter registration drives in the South, the 1963
March on Washington, the Mississippi campaigns,
the national civil rights legislation, the Selma
marches, the struggle for jobs, housing, and
education, and the subsequent explosion of the
ghettos and the emergence of black power and
black separatism. Emboldened by minority
group breakthroughs, as well as the ripening of
their own agendas and strengths, other long-
muted segments of society began to let their
voices be heard. The young took on educational
and military establishments, the poor their welfare bureaucracies, the women their male chau-
vinisms. Old authoritarianisms and oppressions
came under attack everywhere.

While there had always been a conscience
about social injustice in the institutional church
and a small cadre of prophets, in the early part

of the decade of the '60s these formerly marginal forces now got significant support from their own faith community. The established church began to face out toward the Jericho road victims all around it. First it reached timidly to "dialogue" with the world, then finally to confront it head-on. From the coffeehouse and industrial mission that sought to put the church in touch with some of the currents, mission moved into the streets to picket and protest oppressive principalities and powers. Denominational and ecumenical bodies funded controversial programs of social change. A small but vigorous slice of the laity experimented with a new kind of churchmanship that emphasized presence and action in the world. A new breed of clergy, many coming from seminaries where the importance of worldly mission was being encouraged, went into parishes determined to give leadership in civil rights, peace, and poverty areas, or launched para-parochial forms and non-ecclesiastical movements for social change. The shift in the understanding of mission was illustrated by the pilgrimage of Truman Douglass, the author of the earlier church extension-oriented *Mission to America*. Always committed to the social mission of the church, he now gave major accent to this concern, leading his Board for Homeland Ministries into a striking array of involvements and risk-taking ventures running from plunges into the art and counter-culture world of North Beach and Las Vegas to voter registration drives in the deep South and militant community organization in the ghettos of the North.

In the midst of the bend toward the secular, and giving impetus to it, there arose a "theology of the world." Dietrich Bonhoeffer was a dominant influence: a compelling vision of Christ as the "man for others" found expression in a "church for others" (the name of the missionary structure study of the World Council of Churches that had a great impact on denominational rethinking of mission and church retooling in the 1960s).[7] Now was heard the refrain: "God did not die for the church but for the world," and "Go out to meet God where he is working—in the world." Renewal movement texts were heard from again and again: "You are the light of the world," "Go into all the world," and "God so loved the world." Harvey Cox's *Secular City* (selling over 600,000 copies) displaced the Peales and the Liebmans.[8] Fulton Sheen himself spoke less and less of inner peace, and, in his capacity as Bishop of Rochester, more and more of outer justice and even the need for conflict-prone community organization programs. Even Billy Graham mentioned the need for two conversions, the first to Christ and

---

[7] Western European Working Group and North American Working Group, *The Church for Others and the Church for the World* (Geneva: World Council of Churches, 1967).

[8] Harvey Cox, *The Secular City* (New York: Macmillan, 1965).

the second to the world, and integrated his Southern evangelistic rallies.

Renewers and reformers in the church declared that this era was a time of turning. And for important sections of leadership and many constituents, it indeed was—a turning from sacred to secular, from church to world, from "come" to "go." In this period of mission, the congregation became a "go structure."

## Pain and Polarization

As momentum for change in American society increased in the 1960s, the level of conflict deepened and broadened. Resistance began to stiffen in the North as the implication of demands for freedom and justice became increasingly clear; not only Southern de jure segregation was being called into question, but also de facto Northern bigotry. Related inextricably to the resistance, strategies for effecting change escalated from legislative, protest, demonstration, and nonviolent civil disobedience methods to "random violence" in the cities and on the campuses, and the "instrumental violence" of arson, guerrilla warfare, and the rhetoric of revolution. Middle America, identified by angry militants as "white racists," "pigs," "hardhats," and "rednecks," turned upon the agents of change and new life-styles to attack its own stereotypical targets—"hippies," "longhairs," "welfare chiselers," and "uppity niggers." The confrontation took place under flag decals, at the polls, and in the streets.

This cultural push and pull spilled into the churches. New-breed clergy and laity found themselves under heavy attack by an ecclesiastical silent majority. The withholding of funds for innovative and controversial world-oriented programming was early in evidence. New forms and para-parochial ministries were among the first victims of budgetary cutback. Young Turk clergy lost their jobs or chose to drop out in the face of strong parishioner resistance. Congregations were split between traditionalists and visionaries. Underground churches were born, most often to give world-drenched churchmen bases of operation. Caucuses and parties emerged within denominations and local churches, espousing anti-establishment points of view. Clergy unions appeared. Heavy controversy took place in church assemblies about denominational funding, and sedate meetings were confronted by groups of the young, blacks, and women on the one hand, and prayer-in-the-public-schools, *Reader's Digest*-quoting protagonists on the other.

As we all have been partisans in these affrays, we tend to baptize one or the other point of view, seeing the controversy as the "good guys" versus the "bad guys." But for the purpose here of understanding the varying conceptions of mission, it is more accurate to identify the debate as one between different views on the

nature of the church. It is a conflict between
two images of mission: church-oriented and
world-oriented. One group took its signals from
the postwar era, and the other from the revolu-
tions of the '60s. Each is a response to its times,
and a child of its times.

## Beyond Polarization

Now what? Several things are becoming
increasingly clear. One is that the furies within
the church are as suicidal as the factionalism
that rent the Corinthian community. The feud
at Corinth prompted a Pauline letter with its
indictment of narrow visions and its insistence
that diverse ministries be honored, yet within
the context of the wholeness of the Body (I Cor.
12). There is wise counsel there for us. Without
giving up the hard-won commitments and insight
of the past decades, we have to move beyond
internecine strife.

Another clear bell is the call to respond to the
demands of our own time. The '70s are a different era. Old problems persist and in some cases
increase, and past wisdom cannot be lost. But if
we believe that God is at work in the world, we
should be listening for his footfall in our own
Now. Indeed, it may be that attention to the
present mandates of mission, in company with
the things we have learned in the past two eras,
may help us to transcend destructive polarities.
Let us therefore listen for the particular claim

that is being laid upon us, and attend to its implications for the fulness of the Gospel and the wholeness of the church.

## Telling the Story

Whatever else the religious hungers of the young mean (and they do mean other things, which we shall investigate in Ch. 6), the quest for meaning through astrology, Tarot cards, I Ching, Zen, Hare Krishna, Process, Mahareshi, Krishnamurti, and more recently Jesus Christ Superstar and the "Jesus freaks," cannot be ignored by mainline Christianity.[9] The flirtation with the bizarre and exotic is a question put squarely to us: What is your Story? This inquiry comes not only from the young, but from the jaded housewife and the unstrung aerospace engineer looking for some fundamental frame of reference into which this chaotic time and their own life malaise can be put.

If we are to respond to what appears to be a ripe moment for the Story, we have to know it. The sad fact is that our zeal to relate to the cultural demands of earlier epochs has encouraged us not only to mute the message, but also to lose track of it. In the church-centered era of fellowship and existential grapple, we psychologized it. In the era of worldly involvement in the structures of society, we sociologized it. It is

[9] See pp. 79ff.

now time to repossess the theological core that receded before the psychological and sociological claims. We have to recover the full saga of what God did, is doing, and will do.

Peter Berger's tract, *The Noise of Solemn Assemblies* (1961), was part of an early critical literature that questioned the navel-staring into which church-centered mission had fallen, and heralded the era of mission-in-the-world. Ten years later, at his recent address to the COCU Assembly, Berger's sociological perceptions and faith commitment lead him to call for a new "stance of authority."[10] He criticizes the prophets of "relevance" for succumbing to the same cultural accommodation to which their predecessors fell prey in the '50s, although this time it is the counter-culture and chic radical establishments. He urges a move from dialogue to proclamation, from a loss of nerve and too much listening to a forthright telling of the Story. While the same tendency to overstatement that appeared in *The Noise of Solemn Assemblies* is found in this indictment and redirection, Berger is right in affirming the integrity of Christian faith and the need for its articulation. That posture does not mean a new monologue, however, but an authentic dialogue in which there is speaking to as well as hearing from the world.

Can we fulfill our mission mandate to tell the

[10] Peter Berger, "Call for Authority in the Christian Community," *op. cit.*, pp. 1257-1263.

Story without succumbing to the half-truths and
reductionisms to which we have been prone in
other times? So far the signals seem to suggest
that we are being led down the same path of too
easy accommodation to the current cultural
frenzies. Many of the popular and fervent religious stories being told fall short of being the
Story because they neglect fundamental acts in
the drama of God's engagement with his people.
Censored are those chapters that our last two
eras of mission did rediscover: the work of God
in the *church*, and the work of God in the
*world*. Much proclamation about Jesus today is
accommodating too easily to the worst in the
religious quest, retreating to the warm womb of
mystical piety, insulated from the hard institutional challenges of both world and church. If
the Story is told faithfully and accurately, it will
be one of *life with God in a church for the
world.* [11]

How that kind of full-orbed communication
can take place is the top priority on the mission
agenda of the 1970s. Will we be able to find a
way to speak our piece in the very midst of our
struggle with the human issues—at the gates of
Attica, in third-world liberation movements, in
ecological and consumer crusades, in the quest
for peace, in middle-American neighborhoods

---

[11] See Clifford Christians, Earl Schipper, and Wesley Smedes,
*Who in the World?* (Grand Rapids: Eerdmans, 1972), for another
call to put these three themes together ("the truth, the way, and
the life").

and on university campuses? And will we be able to do it not as lone rangers, but as a Christian community of support and sacrament, of prayer and mutual ministry?

If we do, it will be a great time to be alive and in mission. For it will mean that the church-centered and the world-centered will have moved beyond their present impasse to find each other at a rendezvous point out ahead—a place where they have learned together to *tell* and *celebrate* the Tale, and to *do* and *be* it.

## CHAPTER TWO

# A Catechism for Skye: Telling the Tale

*The experience with the Krishnites mentioned earlier, and the contact in Honolulu with fervent devotees of other new religions, prompted this attempt to capsule the main points of the Christian faith. As one of the writer's teen-age daughters, Skye, was at this time preparing for church membership, the effort took shape as a catechetical dialogue.*

*Question*: Peter Townsend has given his testimony to Meher Baba in "Rolling Stone," the Beatles have told us about their gurus, many others are into Zen, astrology, or even witchcraft. And now Jesus Christ is coming on strong as a Superstar. The ordinary church, St. John's-by-the-gas-station, seems to be terribly out of it in all this. Does it have anything to say?

*Answer*: It's true, we haven't been talking much lately about what makes us tick. We've

been too busy—either arguing about the cost of
the new signboard in front of the church, or
starting a coffeehouse for the kids. We should
really be ashamed of the time we waste on
adorning our buildings while the world is burning. But as far as the coffeehouse goes and other
attempts to care about people who have needs
or are hurting—that's the kind of help for victims on the Jericho road that the church is
supposed to be up to. After all, Christ didn't tell
the Good Samaritan to hand out a tract or hold
a seance. The Bible says the stranger "bound up
wounds." But it is true that, alongside our acts
of compassion and struggle for justice and peace,
we have to communicate what we believe. We
must try to answer the question that Superstar
puts in Judas' mouth, "I only want to
know. . . ." People today are agonizing about
questions of life and death, God and man. It's
time to tell our story.

### The Story Begins

*Question*: Tell your story? That doesn't
sound like a philosophical trip or a lesson in
meditation.

*Answer*: That is one of the things that makes
Christianity different. It is a tale about something that has happened, is happening, and will
happen.

The drama unfolds like this: "In the begin-

ning . . ." God had a dream.[1] A dream of a
world that gave back the love that God "himself" is (until we get better words that clean up
the male domination of our language, we reluc-
tantly use "he" and "man" in talking about God
and humanity). Donald Baillie, the Scottish
theologian, captures it in his picture of a campfire surrounded by a circle of exuberant dancers.[2] Their eyes are on the fire, their arms are
linked, and the glow cast on the trees around is
warm and friendly. The fire is God, the dancers
are humanity, the environment is nature. It is a
world at one with itself.

If the dream was to come true, if Love was to
be answered by love, man would have to return
it as freely as God gave it. Friendship with God
can't be programmed. So a key figure in the
drama was made like God—in the code language
of the Bible, in the "image of God." Man was
born with a capacity to say "yes" or "no" to his
Maker.

The plot thickens. The creature with the
human face didn't turn out as hoped. He was
much more interested in himself than in God.
Human beings—symbolized in the biblical saga
by the figure Adam (which means mankind)—

[1] The author has attempted to develop these themes in greater
detail in *Humiliation and Celebration* (New York: Sheed and
Ward, 1969) and *The Rainbow Sign* (Grand Rapids: Eerdmans,
1969), and for church discussion groups in *Conversation in Faith*
(Philadelphia: United Church, 1968).
[2] Donald Baillie, *God Was in Christ* (New York: Scribner's,
1948), pp. 205-206. See also *Conversation in Faith, op. cit.*, pp.
46f.

turned on their heels away from God, and for that matter their fellow humans, and nature as well. To go back to our campfire, the dancers wheeled around with their backs to the blaze. That back-turning is what the code word "sin" means. Its result is the breaking of arms linked with others. So we now have a scene in which lonely figures who can't see each other anymore face an outer darkness illumined only by fearsome shadows cast by their frantic and lonely gyrations. Here is the plight of our world, according to the Christian Story. The estrangement of humans from God, from each other, and from nature. It is the killing of the dream—God's dream.

Now another act in the drama opens. The Dreamer is not going to leave it at that. He scatters hints and clues of his intentions throughout the whole human race—deep in the conscience of people, in the ups and downs of nations, in the beauty and rhythms of nature. He does not leave himself "without witness." The starry heavens above, the conscience within, the lessons learned in the rise and fall of nations—all work together to call humanity to something better.

But all this doesn't turn man around. Something more drastic is needed.

## A Gift: The Vision of Shalom

The hoping God then fixes upon a small Near Eastern tribe noted for its stubborn and stiff-necked ways. If it can happen here, it can happen anywhere. God makes a "covenant" with Israel.

This people will experience the unswerving, patient pull of God toward his dream by their pilgrimage from slavery to a Promised Land. Further, God will give them a clear idea of the kind of response he expects from that act of generosity—the moral commandments of right and wrong. In response they will be asked to love God back and serve his cause.

So God does his part. He takes them out of Egyptian slavery into a land flowing with milk and honey. He raises up leaders like Moses who spell out the right and wrong of things. On top of that there come prophets who keep reminding people of the covenant, and who sketch a picture of what the world would look like if it were finally together, *shalom,* a vision of liberation and reconciliation among God, man, and nature.[3] In that world all the fractures are finally healed: between man and God, man and man, man and nature, within nature, and among man, nature, and God. Swords are beaten into plowshares, the wolf and lamb lie down together, the child puts her hand over the snake's hole, and every man dwells under his vine and fig tree.

No go. The effort fails, as the chosen people keep acting like the rest of humanity.

[3] The meaning of shalom is explored in *The Church for Others, op. cit.,* pp. 14ff.; J. Verkuyl, *The Message of Liberation in Our Age* (Grand Rapids: Eerdmans, 1972), pp. 18-19 and *passim;* and the July-August 1972 issue of *Colloquy.*

## God Himself Had to Make the Scene

So what's left to do? One thing. God himself is going to have to make the scene. Evil has such a grip on the race that something more powerful than human will power is going to have to deal with it.

Dealing with evil involves several things. For one, it means breaking the grip it has on people; for another, showing unmistakably what an alternative life-style would look like; and for still another, not just ignoring the hurt caused by humanity's disobedience, but paying up for it.

So the Story tells us that God enters the picture, the hurly-burly arena of human guilt and grief. He doesn't arrive with jets, napalm, atomic hardware, and forty-five divisions of tanks. He comes as one ordinary workingman. This Jesus is no superstar, but a teller of stories, a doer of deeds, a healer of hurts. In all the doing, telling, and healing, it begins to dawn on the people close to him—the "disciples"—that this is a very different way of life. He is not a person out for himself, but a "man for others."

The world of lonely dancers can't stand having such a person around showing them up. They have to get rid of him. They turn him into a criminal and execute him by the cruelest method available.

But something else happened in this event than the dispensing of just one more visionary. Remember, the Story tells us that they were dealing with God, or "the Son of God."

## God Took a Beating for Us

By nailing Jesus to a cross, man was executing the logic of God's own plan to make his dream come true. That crucifixion was the only way God could show humans what was really in his mind and heart—long-suffering love. And its pain demonstrated the cost to God for man's betrayal of the hope of shalom. There is no cheap forgiveness. God's broken heart is the price paid for our turning away. The "anger" we so much deserve for our rebuff of his friendship is overcome in God himself by his mercy. God takes the beating for us, so to speak. That is what it means to say "Christ died for our sins."

But there is more to come.

The grip of evil in which the world is held is broken. The strange spell cast over the dancers that turns them from the Light is ended. Death—separation from God—is over on Easter morning. The resurrection of Jesus is more than the revival of a dead body. Easter is a sign and seal that we are no longer under the sway of what the Bible calls "the principalities and powers." Shalom can be! God's hope will happen. The "kingdom of God" will come.

## A New Ball Game and a New Ball Club

This heavy transaction that takes place in the life, teaching, death, and resurrection of Jesus is the hinge of history. After it, things are differ-

ent. There's a new ball game. The world is
"Christic," alive with the presence of hope, open
to new possibilities because the powers of evil
no longer run riot. True, as long as the world
exists, egotism and evil will be busy corrupting
the best spurts forward humans can make, for
this is earth we live in, not heaven. The kingdom
will come only in God's good time—the last
chapter of the Story. But the Storytellers see the
world they now live in with a new pair of eyes.
They can "discern the signs" of Christ's presence
in it, tracing the hints of shalom that God brings
into our world wherever there are struggles and
victories for peace and freedom—within man,
between humans, among nations, in nature, and
with God. Where there are such signs of hope we
have the "fruits of the Spirit."

Just as there is a new ball game, there is a new
ball club. That is the fruit of the Spirit, too. A
"new Israel," the church, is called into being to
report the happenings surrounding Jesus, to
embody Jesus' life-style in its own communities,
and to live it out in the world as agents of
reconciliation and instruments of liberation. The
church is a "tomorrow people," lured on by the
vision of shalom that God projects on the screen
of the future. What gives them hope is that
they've seen the dream take on reality in Jesus.
And that same future, and its breakthrough in
Christ, also gives them a sense of urgency about
doing something to show people what the vision
is all about. They are pilgrims and strangers to

the status quo of slavery, injustice, untruth, hate, and hurt, determined to set up signposts to the dream of shalom in this world.

## Signposts

*Question*: Well, what are these signposts? What is the life-style that comes from believing the Story?

*Answer*: Paul, one of the first organizers of the new communities, wrote some important letters to these early Christians which are preserved in the Storybook. He did it to advise the early congregations about their new posture. He summed it up in three words: faith, hope, love.

*Faith* is our personal response to the Story. Faith is betting our life on the God who reaches out to us in its happenings. It is trust in the relentless love that bounds toward us through these events. And it's a penitent trust in the suffering love that accepts us in our unacceptability. This kind of faith is kept warm and vital by the life of prayer—confession, thanksgiving, petition, intercession, covenant, adoration.

*Hope* is our stance toward the yet-to-be-told Tale. Based on faith in what God has done and is doing, hope orients toward what God promises he will do. Hope is the confidence that God will be waiting for us with his offer of shalom in our every tomorrow, and the assurance of its fulfillment in a Great Tomorrow. Hope is "aiglatson," forward nostalgia, or appetite whetted for the not-yet.

*Love* is the child of faith and hope. It is care for the things that God cares for, and keeping close to the stirrings toward shalom for which hope looks and longs. It is compassion for the weak and the hurt, the neighbor in need, as the parable of the Good Samaritan explains (our neighbor, the green earth, as well as our human neighbors). Most of all, human love strives to reflect God's love, to do good to those who do us in. So a Christian life-style covers the clock. Grounded in the events that surround Christ, it is past-oriented. Moving out to love and to serve the neighbor in need, it is present-oriented. Lured by the God who meets us at a rendezvous point out ahead, it is future-oriented. Faith, love, hope—these three. And the greatest of these is love.

## What's Love Got to Do with My Life?

*Question:* What does this love and love's Story have to do with where people live—the day-to-day hassles and hangups, the headlines of our newspaper, what we do when we get up in the morning or where we go out at night?

*Answer:* It makes all the difference in the world. If you bet your life on it, you know who you are, how to make some sense of the events around you, and what you are called to do about them. Take a hot issue—the struggle for justice by VLPs (Very Little Persons who have been submerged by VIPs), the poor, the black, the young, women, aged, consumers, middle Americans.

From the *beginning* of the Story, we get the call to treat every human being with dignity because each is made in the image of God. As that image includes the freedom to choose, Story-believers will struggle for the right of every human to have a say in his or her own destiny, and to be liberated from any tyrannies that stand in the way of that God-given right.

From the *middle* of the Story—Jesus—we get a confirmation of that call in his life for others, and a particular emphasis on the dignity of victims who have been put down (the Jericho road).

From the *End* of the Story—shalom, the kingdom of God—we get the pull of a vision that does not settle for liberation alone. Here is a dream of a world in which people are not only free to be, but free to be together. Reconciliation is the companion and crown of liberation.

*Question*: Isn't it easy to concentrate so much on the horizontal issues—on secular affairs—that the vertical things threaten to get lost from view? How does the "religious" dimension of the Story fit in here?

*Answer*: Our world with its technological power has raised the stakes in the game of life— it has made the hurts much more perilous and the hopes more promising. Wars are not fought with bows and arrows, but with napalm that can incinerate a village or atomic hardware that can destroy a metropolis. On the other hand, food

and medical miracles make possible undreamed-
of new life for millions. These capacities, and
the abuse of them, focus the attention of a
shalom-oriented Story on how much liberation
and reconciliation its tellers have to *do* as well as
*tell* about.

But the saga may indeed get lost in the shuffle
if we concentrate only on the *doing* to the
exclusion of the *telling* and the *celebrating*. It's
that flinging of the faith in the air joyfully that
has to be recovered now in the midst of our
effort at doing the deeds.

*Question*: Who tells and celebrates the Story?

*Answer*: One community, marked by the sign
of baptism, is called to keep alive the memories
and hopes that surround Jesus—the church. The
congregation at the corner of Fifth and Maple
may be nothing much to write home about. But
it is doing something nobody else is. It is the
custodian of the Story and of its Storybook.
That makes it a group of Storytellers. In the
very conventional things that go on—teaching
third-graders about Jesus, listening to a sermon
that has been sweat over by a dedicated minister, singing songs, sending its money to its
denomination to keep its mission going at home
and abroad, rapping about life and death in a
youth group, women's guild, or churchmen's
brotherhood, breaking bread and drinking wine,
baptizing, confirming, marrying, burying—in
these actions and events the Tale is told and
celebrated.

To be what it is, the Body of Christ, the

church must get its weary bones in motion walking and working in the world. But even in its stumbling state, it is still the Body of which Christ is the Head. If God is big enough to keep company with it, we can do no less.

## Getting the Show "On the Road"

*Question*: How do you put together the Christian's work in the world and his work in the church?

*Answer*: The Storybook says that after the resurrection Jesus was traveling to Emmaus and met two disciples. They didn't recognize him, but their conversation was so intense that "their hearts burned within them." Later, at a meal, "in the breaking of bread," he made himself known to them.

So it is today. There are two kinds of relationship that Christ sustains with people. "On the road"—in day-to-day dealings with people, Christ is present. But he comes incognito, as the unknown friend ministering wherever the hungry are fed, the naked are clothed, and the prisoner visited (Matt. 25). Those people who help the helpless, make peace and do justice, unintentionally serve Christ in those acts. He is their unknown companion.

On other occasions, Christ is met face-to-face. He reveals himself at the Table—we know him in holy communion, prayer, and in the life together of the Christian community, the church.

Here he breaks his silence to speak his word and name his name.

The tragedy among church people is that they so often see only one kind of relationship with Christ—either on the road in the world, or in the room in the church.

If those in the Christian community who hear the Story do not follow the Christ whom they see there onto the Emmaus and Jericho roads, they may find their churches suffering and dying for lack of contact with their Source.

On the other hand, if those who give their all in acts of healing and justice couldn't care less about the Christ who offers his personal life, there is a tragic incompleteness to their bond with Christ. He remains the stranger.

The fulness of relationship is one in which the Christ of the road and the Christ of the room is served and known in world and in church.

## When Religion Gets Personal

*Question*: Have we really gotten down to the deepest level yet? The new religions stress an individual's own experience and feelings as the most important thing.

*Answer*: It is true that we have not touched bottom until we get personal about faith. We put if off this long because Christianity is basically the biography of God, not our own spiritual autobiography. To think first and foremost of our own tale is to get into a kind of navel-gazing in which we still are trapped in "I, me, and mine." But the goal of God's action remains unreached until *his* Story becomes *our* story. You and I were there right in the middle of those campfire back-turners, and there again "when they crucified my Lord," and we are there now when the word comes, "choose this day whom you will serve." Faith is more than belief that the Tale is true. It's trust that it is true for *me*.

The religious search on today is trying to tell us that there is more to religion than just a head trip or a foot trip, all talk or all action. Of course, Christian faith doesn't go along with the mindlessness and copping out that characterizes much of faddish mysticism. But genuine faith has got to be personal and real—a *soul* trip. Being a Christian is having soul, soul that can descend to the quiet depths in meditation and fly high in acts of celebration. Its rhythms are born from the ways of God himself, who is a Pilgrim of crucifixion and resurrection, humiliation and exaltation. Personal faith is a response to who God is, who we are, and what we must do. Or better, it is learning with God *to be*, knowing how in the stillnesses and in the soarings to "let it be."

## The Rings of Faith

*Question*: How do you know your faith is right and the Story true?

*Answer*: The Story has its own way of convincing. You might say that the chief Character himself steps out of its pages to confirm it. But for that to happen we have to position ourselves, like an outfielder who moves over to where the batter is most likely to hit the ball.

The passage to that place is through a series of concentric circles. At the center is God. Close in is the ring of the Gospel, the Story of what God did, is doing, and will do. The adjacent circle is the home of the Story, the Storybook, the Bible in whose pages the drama unfolds. Next out is the orbit of those who bear the Book, the community of Storytellers, the church. On the outer rim is Storyland, the world in which men work and play, love and hate, read and write, laugh and cry, live and die.

The way to God is down the cone: a life with soul immersed deeply in the land of hope and hurt, keeping company with a band of pilgrims squinting at their guidebook with its centerfold map. So we seek the Lord of the rings. And so we are found by him.

## CHAPTER THREE

# Obedience and Trust

How is Story-telling carried out without falling prey to the Babylonian captivity of popular religion? Some of Dietrich Bonhoeffer's searching observations on cheap grace take on special meaning today. It is worth meditating on one of his thought-provoking epigrams: "Only those who obey believe; only those who believe obey."[1]

Today's religious urges and surges reach eagerly for belief and have little to say about or do with obedience. It seems that the obvious corrective to that is to add the love of neighbor to the love of God. But there is a more profound problem here than the need to substitute a both/and for an either/or. "Obey-believe" is a paradox, not simply a partnership. One can't come into being without the other. There can be no authentic faith outside of obedience; obedi-

[1] Dietrich Bonhoeffer, *The Cost of Discipleship* (New York: Macmillan, 1961), pp. 58ff.

ence must be grounded in and informed by
faith.

*Only those who obey believe*. All the piety in
the world, complete with fervent prayer, Scrip-
ture quotations, smiling testimonies, rafter-
ringing hymnody, pulpit-pounding, and exuberant tongue speaking, is no assurance of Gospel
faith. "Not every one who says to me, 'Lord,
Lord,' shall enter the kingdom of heaven." What
distinguishes true belief from false religion? "He
who does the will of my Father who is in
heaven." Faith happens in pilgrimage along the
Jericho roads. Note, however: to put feet on
those paths guarantees no one a route into the
kingdom. We are not saved by works but by
faith that comes from encounter with the Word.
What doing does is position us for the hearing.
We come into earshot of Jesus Christ when we
keep company with him where he is. According
to the twenty-fifth chapter of Matthew that
Presence is to be found among the hungry and
the hurt. How can there be a genuine hearing of
his Word by a religion that distances itself from
the Christ who is ministering to the prisoner, the
stranger, and the poor? And compounds this
alienation from Jesus by scorning such efforts as
"humanism," "the social gospel," "modern-
ism"? Indeed, the interpretation of these actions
by a trivialized theology may be just that. But
the actions themselves are not. They put us
alongside the Presence. The Bible is a book that
opens itself to pilgrims who are in the company

of the serving Christ. Faith comes alive in the midst of those movements of obedience and neighbor love that seek to bind up the wounds of today's victims. The Christian Story must be told and heard by people on a pilgrimage through these lands of oppression and hope.

Because of the obey-believe paradox, the recent plunge of mainstream churches into the human issues—their "much" involvement in "mission to the world"—and our society's preoccupation with these issues position them for good hearing and telling. Luther came to faith by way of good works, and before him, Paul. A secular Christianity caught up in action ministries in the world will sooner or later be faced with the same perplexities that Paul and Luther confronted—"I do not do the good I want, but the evil I do not want is what I do. . . . Wretched man that I am!" Any deadly serious effort in obedience must finally come up against virtue's divided mind and will, the temptations to self-righteousness of the "good," the sin that can be covered only by the divine mercy, and the obstinate surd of evil in the world whose final demise is only assured by the divine promise. The grasp of these profound levels of penitence and faith comes by wrestling with the law. For the law to be schoolmaster, the student must be enrolled in the course. Whether an activist era can learn those lessons and be moved to share them is yet to be determined. But in its involvement it has indeed been a student in a school of hard knocks. Faith is not a high grade earned in that kind of curriculum; it comes by grace. Yet that struggle does put the learner alongside the Teacher and in range of his wisdom.

The tragedy of the current religious boom is that it is more a flight from good works than a way through works to faith. A faddish neo-mysticism leaves behind action and involvement for a thoroughly unbiblical retreat from the world, productive of neither faith nor works. The law as schoolmaster? School is out for the new religiosity. How can belief be born when there are no lessons in obedience? The answers of faith make sense only to those who know the questions. And the schoolmaster puts those to us in his Jericho road curriculum. Perhaps only as the present pietism gives way to a new world-liness will we have the right context for the recovery of faith. Only those who obey believe.

*Only those who believe obey*. There are "is" and "ought" dimensions to this end of the paradox. On the one hand, the affirmation describes how things in fact do shape up. On the other, it points to how they ought to be.

Levi's response to Jesus' terse word to leave his business and follow him (Mark 2:14) was an obedience that presupposed trust. Obedience indeed preceded the full bloom of devotion that was yet to come in his relationship to Christ, but the seeds of faith were already there in the initial act of loyalty.

The same Jesus, now incognito, puts the same question to every decider confronted with the choice for or against the neighbor's need. The hidden Christ of Matthew 25 comes to us in each claim made upon us by the wretched of the earth. Those choices to hurt or heal, to turn aside from or bend down over, the victims of our time are invariably related to Jesus. The contemporary act of obedience, like that of Levi, is at the same time an act of faith. It represents the belief that there is something in the nature of things that supports compassion, the worship of "an unknown God." Thus, unaware of it, the one who obeys ministers through the victim to Christ himself. The act is a sign of implicit faith. "He who loves is born of God and knows God."

Implicit faith is fine as far as it goes, but God wills maturity. We are called to grow from milk to solid food, from birth to the full stature of Christ. Coming of age means the end of groping for the hidden Christ to receiving the One who reveals himself at Bethlehem, in Galilee and Calvary, and on Easter morning. Belief, in the deepest sense, is an act of the spirit that comes to terms with this disclosure. It is being caught by the vision of the kingdom that Christ portrays and is; broken by our failure to pursue this dream and the horror of our titanic assault upon it; rescued from the misery of this breach by a suffering Love that covers our lovelessness; and alerted to a promise that the powers of sin and evil cannot finally defeat his shalom.

This kind of belief makes a difference in obedience. For one, it shatters the complacency of obeyers who have never plumbed the depths of ambiguity in their own good works. For another, when the Christian Tale strikes home, it really strikes home; it turns people around (*metanoia*), away from the I, me, and mine and out toward God and neighbor. Those who believe are set on the way to obey.

As hearts are broken open by faith, so are minds. Belief ranges through the documents that brought it to be for light on the acts of obedience to which it is called. Theology, the Christian community's reflection on the biblical events, is belief's instrument of discernment. The shape obedience must take in a particular time comes clear by dialogue with the fathers and brethren, the mothers and sisters, of faith. Theology is the act of thinking together about how the Story sheds light upon the issues of peace and war, race and ethnicity, poverty and affluence, ecology and ecumenism. Belief lights a candle for the dark passageways of contemporary decision. Those who believe can better obey.

## Telling and Doing

As faith is costly, so too there is no cheap telling. The growing conviction that the Story

must be told with fresh power is to be wel-
comed. But that telling has to be joined to
costly choices. Obedience-less talk is the mother
of bad faith. The speaker helps the hearer attend
to the Word when he takes him along to its
place of lively Presence in the world. Trust and
obey, there is no other way.

## CHAPTER FOUR

# Engagement Evangelism

To believe that the Story must be told in the setting of today's events is one thing. Knowing how to do it is quite another. In this chapter we explore some ways in which that kind of mating can happen. We look particularly at the kind of Christian communication that goes out from the church toward the world—evangelism, sharing with others "the wonderful deeds" of God. Our proposals have implications too for other kinds of Tale-bearing carried on within the life of the Christian community (for example, the nurture that takes place in teaching and preaching), but we do not pursue them here, except indirectly in our examination of the "enclave" idea.[1]

---

[1] An "action-reflection" methodology is widely discussed in circles of church and theological education. See, for example, Robert Bonthius, "Theological Education for Revolutionary Response," mimeograph, 1969, and Robert Burt, Issue-Action kit, Division of Christian Education, United Church of Christ, 1971.

Two things happen when the evangel strikes home: (1) It evokes commitment. A sluice gate opens and there is flooding of the parched lands of the spirit. (2) It lights up old darknesses. Fresh vistas appear. New understanding is born.

The first is a change of heart, the second a change of head. In the language of another time, one is "fiducia," the other "assensus"—trust and belief. Together they comprise faith, a turning around of soul and mind.

Evangelism is getting the Word out so that this faith might come to be. *Engagement* evangelism is a telling inextricably bound up with a doing. It is a movement to the yonder places of involvement where the Spirit consummates the union of trust and obedience.

The further places, the sites of worldly fear and hope where faith can come alive, are of two kinds, those given and those designed.

*The Given.* There are great events and historical stirrings within whose shadow the telling and celebrating of the Story become natural and compelling. The struggles for justice and peace in the last decade became such an environment: Martin Luther King, Jr., preaching on the eve of a dangerous march; Kilmer Meyer offering bread and wine on the steps of a segregated church; prayers of intercession rising from a jail cell; rich biblical symbols of swords and plowshares, vine and fig tree, lifted up in a town square on a peace vigil. All of these testimonies, made countless times in struggles toward liberation and reconciliation, often unintended as such, are ways of engagement evangelism. The dream of shalom is portrayed homiletically and liturgical-ly in the midst of shalom-affirming realities. And the Word did its work, for hearts and minds were changed, decisions made, visions seen.

This blowing of the Spirit cannot be contrived by the plans of men. It is given. The most we can do is attempt to discern the signs of such times, find our way into the thick of them, and when pressed by the circumstances be ready to give reasons for the hope that is in us.

*The Chosen.* There is a meeting of evangel and circumstance in which the design of the evange-list plays a greater role. A larger historical hand still sets the stage by bringing to the fore the action issues. But the way these issues are dealt with is shaped by those who seek to fuse faith and obedience.

A long-forgotten evangelical constituency is available for this work. Who is better positioned for action evangelism than those who are daily actors? If the fundamental theater of evangelism is the world, then the 99 percent of the Chris-tian community who live there—the laity—seem the natural bearers of tidings. Here is the arena, and here are the participants who must face the critical questions of war and peace, poverty and affluence, hate and love.

An older "theology of the laity" brought forcefully home the neglect and significance of the people of God with its secular presence and

calling. The role of the clergy came to be seen as
that of equipping these troops for their mission
in the world.[2]

The "discovery" of the laity was an important
step in grasping the nature of the church. In an
era in which mission was interpreted primarily in
terms of action in the world, it was inevitable
that the vocation of laity be thought of as commensurate with servanthood: laymen and lay-
women are the arms and legs of the Body in the
world. However, as our understanding of mission
widens to include telling too, the perception of
lay calling must also be broadened. The laity are
bearers of the word as well as the deed.

Here we must avoid a fatal misstep, one that
ignores all we have learned about the special gift
of the laity. The danger is the threat of a cleri-
calized conception of lay witness that severs the
teller from the doing that defines his or her very
life. Consider two forms of this cleavage: (1) a
tract-wielding, button-holing evangelism devoid
of any connection with the time, place, or issues
in which confronted and confronter are immersed;[3] (2) a doorbell-ringing evangelism in
which sorties are made for ecclesiastical aggran-

[2] Hendrik Kraemer, *A Theology of the Laity* (Philadelphia:
Westminster, 1959), is a definitive work, with Hans-Rudi Weber's
*Salty Christians* (New York: Seabury, 1962) being a popular
study book on similar themes.

[3] For a criticism of this kind of "lapel evangelism" as well as
its extreme opposite, "incognito evangelism," see the author's
*Secular Impact* (Philadelphia: United Church, 1968), pp. 12-21.

dizement with no recognition of the hopes and
fears that lie behind the portals. In both cases
there is, by the sin of omission, scorn for the
reality of the laity as actors in the world.

How then is the melding of Tale and time to
be done? Let us examine two models in which
the reality of the laity is affirmed in engagement
evangelism: the *enclave* and the *conclave*.

*Enclave*. "The equipping of the saints for the
work of ministry" is a familiar concept from the
period of lay renewal (Eph. 4:11-12). Within the
life of the Christian community, laity are trained
to exercise their ministry in the world. The
ordained members of the people of God serve as
equippers and resources. An enclave model of
engagement evangelism builds upon this insight.
The Story is brought to bear on the crises and
possibilities of the contemporary world with a
view to expanding the horizons and deepening
the commitment of the learner, so that the laity
may in turn share these perceptions in their own
circle of involvement. The issues may run from
unemployment, nuclear war, ecological disaster,
and ethnic consciousness to abortion, marriage,
and biomedical engineering. The hard data about
these matters are brought by those who daily
live with them—the workers, draftees, consumers, mothers, husbands, students, secretaries,
militants, doctors, teachers, welfare recipients,
and bank managers who compose the reality of
the laity. The clergy (who, of course, also have
their secular credentials in more than a few of

these involvements) do not hand down answers
to these questions. They bring into the dialogue
about them the theological training and experience peculiar to their calling (again not entirely
exclusive to them as many laity have some of
the same). In the give and take, fresh horizons of
meaning begin to emerge. A growth of mind and
spirit happens that is destined to communicate
itself beyond the boundaries of the enclave.

The enclave becomes a launching pad for
evangelism to the degree that the perceptions
won there are shared by the individual lay mis-
sioner at the places, and among the people, of
similar concern. Telling the Story in such set-
tings does not mean "laying on" another the
heavy burden of sloganeering God-talk. It is
speaking about God naturally in the act of
engagement with a human issue, often (although
not always) because you are asked why you view
it, or do it, that way and not another. Any
profound grapple with a burning issue must
finally press to the point where questions about
the nature of man and God and the meaning of
life, death, and destiny are confronted. It is then
that the training that has taken place within the
life of the Christian community must demonstrate whether it has in fact been "an equipping
of the saints for the work of ministry."

*Conclave.* Since frontier days the revival-
meeting has been the familiar corporate expression of evangelism outside the walls of the congregation. Here we examine another way of

assembling to speak about God on worldly turf,
one that tries to take seriously the rumbles and
quakes in that terrain. We call it a "conclave"
because it seeks to bring together the people of
the church and the people of the world, in
contrast to the confessing community that
makes up the enclave. Thus outreach is in tandem with inreach for the work of engagement
evangelism.

Those who gather in conclave come, first and
foremost, to probe a vital human issue. As before, the questions may range from Archie Bunker to Zero Population Growth. However, the
ground rules of such an exploration require
penetration far below the surface. Participants
understand that ultimate questions as well as
penultimate ones will be addressed. Conventional secular inquiries about the same matters may
rule out of order the discussion of the religious,
philosophical, and even moral dimensions of
such questions ("they are divisive"; "let's deal
with the nuts and bolts, not a lot of speculation"; "our business is to stick to the how and
not bother about the why," etc.). But there will
be no such pragmatist and technician mentality
limits set for conclave inquiry. Those who work
along the horizontal route of human issues ac-
knowledge that they will be traveling vertical
trails as well, that man-man issues merge into
man-God ones.

Laity who have been equipped for their ministry will participate in these probes because they

are looking for a way to deal with the human
crisis or opportunity addressed there, because
they believe that faith can illumine these issues,
and because they are moved to share their fundamental commitments with those seeking
meaning in life. It is on these terms and in this
context of secular obedience that the Story can
come alive.

We have called this type of evangelism
"chosen" rather than "given." The church can
create the arena in which its message can take on
form and life. Instead of the conventional structures of mass evangelism, it can design conclaves
around a current issue, making provision for the
kind of digging that will get to the ultimates,
encouraging the setting forth of different per-
spectives at that level, and seeing to it that the
Christian Story is represented by involved laity.

As our interpretation of lay Storytellers has
its antecedent in an earlier theology of the laity,
so too conclave evangelism has its forerunner in
a concept of lay mission from the same era. The
"Evangelical Academy" born in the reconstruction period of postwar Europe was a sensitive
effort to bring the resources of the Christian
faith and community to bear on the social and
political issues of that time, and subsequent
ones.[4] As with the conception of laity that arose
then, so too in the case of the Academy, resolu-
tion of the human issue was the focus of mis-

[4] Franklin Littell, *The German Phoenix* (Garden City, N. Y.:
Doubleday, 1960).

sion, with faith and the ministrations of the faith community justified only to the extent they contributed to that end. Further, the presence of faith was viewed essentially in terms of theological or ethical wisdom that might contribute to the enlightenment of the participants (hence an "academy"). Here again we must begin with former insights and build upon them. Together with the focus on the issue, which the Academy stressed, there must be a press below to root religious questions, one that not only deals with theological themes but touches down as well on profoundly personal aspects. And more, in the conclave, initiative for this testimony is in the hands of the laity themselves, not theological specialists or pastors, as is regularly the case in the Academy model.

Evangelism in conclave form is an alternative to the evangelistic rally. In one case the invitation to find God is given by passage through the world, in the other by circumventing it. In such a workshop of the Gospel all sorts and conditions of men can learn anew about an incarnate Word that is to be heard and seen in the world. Engagement evangelism needs some pilot ventures in these new directions just as surely as other ages raised up their missionary pioneers.

Before we take up a specific case of engagement evangelism, passing mention should be made of an exercise in witnessing that appears to be what we have been describing but in fact is not. It is found among "Jesus people" who attach themselves to public events and actions. Thus the Children of God will be found at a peace rally with their signs and sighs, or the followers of a charismatic young evangelist will be seen distributing tracts at a demonstration for welfare rights, another group will have its booth at a rock festival, and still another will join with its own placards a picket line protesting discrimination. The difference between these attachments and engagement evangelism is the presence of obedience. Both are on the Jericho road, but one is there as priest attending to pious duties and the other is there to minister to the victim. One exploits the presence of the activist; the other becomes one, and seeks to undergird the action with faith. One is an appendage evangelism that fixes itself to a living situation but is not part of it. The other is an integral evangelism woven into the cloth of life. "Only those who obey believe."

## CHAPTER FIVE

# Middle America: Agenda for Engagement Evangelism

Engagement evangelism must do its work in the midst of the issues of the '70s. One that has come to the fore in the last few years, and promises to be with us for some time to come, is *middle America*. It can serve as a laboratory for the blending of doing and telling. Middle America is a "given" historical phenomenon not unlike that of the struggle for black identity and power, even though its present surface manifestations suggest that it is an attempt to counter the advance of minority rights. The Christian community needs some well-"chosen" enclaves and conclaves that deal with the meaning of this phenomenon. It touches directly many of its own constituents and will significantly affect the political and social direction of the United States. Ultimately the church will have to relate itself to the liberation struggle of middle Americans as it has done in the past with other aggrieved sections of the society. Let us see how the Story can illumine the question, and in the dialogue emerge as a powerful and personal Tale.

In 1972 "Archie Bunker for President" booths appeared in department stores around the country. The pop buttons, posters, and bumper stickers were spillovers from the nation's number one television program, "All in the Family."

Many commentators interpreted this craze as the escalation of racism and jingoism. There in all its ugliness was Archie's crude prejudice and putdown of dissenters. Others, however, saw something behind the bigotry: a new self-awareness and identity quest on the part of large constituencies of working-class and lower-middle-class citizens. For them flag-waving seemed to be less a call to arms and more a distress signal. Robert Coles explored these themes in *The Middle Americans*, and Jack Newfield and Jeff Greenfield drew up a charter for their aspirations in *The Populist Manifesto*. At the outset of the decade *Time, Newsweek,* and other mass media took note of them. And then middle America began to make its own presence felt in the populist sentiments expressed in the 1972 Democratic primaries.[1]

[1] For background to this chapter see Gabriel Fackre, *Liberation in Middle America* (Philadelphia: United Church, 1971) and "Archie Bunker: Visions and Realities," *The Christian Century*, Vol. LXXXIX, No. 27 (July 19, 1972), pp. 772-774. There is a growing literature on middle America. In addition to the works to which direct reference will later be made, these pioneering studies should be mentioned: Jack Newfield and Jeff

As we begin our exploration, let us get out data that will have a bearing on where we go, some of the *facts* and some of the *faith*. (1) Matters of fact: Middle America is a segment of the nation described by Scammon and Wattenberg in *The Real Majority* as "unyoung, unpoor, and unblack."[2] We interpret the middling unyoung (unold, too) to be those citizens roughly between thirty and sixty years of age. In-between Americans are unrich as well as unpoor, having incomes in the range of five thousand to fifteen thousand dollars a year. The unblack are also unred, unyellow, and unbrown; they are among the "white majority."[3] Middle Americans work in factories and offices, and live in blue-collar ethnic neighborhoods in the city, and in white-collar WASP suburbias. There are about eighty million of them. (2) Matters of faith: The Story reveals God's dream—shalom—and the assault upon it by the human race; God's dialogue with man about this alienation in the covenant history of Israel and in the larger landscape; his

Greenfield, *The Populist Manifesto* (New York: Paperback Library, 1971); Robert Coles and Jon Erikson, *The Middle Americans* (Boston: Little, Brown, 1971); Richard Lemon, *The Troubled American* (New York: Simon and Schuster, 1970); James Armstrong, *Mission: Middle America* (Nashville: Abingdon, 1971); Kenneth Lasson, *The Workers*, afterword by Ralph Nader (New York: Grossman, 1971); Arthur Shostak, *Blue Collar Life* (New York: Random, 1969); Peter Binzen, *Whitetown, USA* (New York: Random, 1970).

[2] Richard Scammon and Ben Wattenberg, *The Real Majority* (New York: Coward-McCann, 1970).

[3] Louise Kapp Howe, *The White Majority* (New York: Random, 1970).

appearance on the scene in Jesus to embody the vision, to take upon himself the pain and guilt of the breach and give the coup de grace to the destructive powers; the ensuing birth of the telling and doing community that points to signs of the dream in the world and the promise of its fulfillment.

Visionaries with their eyes opened to shalom by its coming in Jesus are newly sighted. Martin Luther King had that kind of "eschatological" eyes (able to see "future and final things"). In his memorable speech at the Lincoln Memorial, "I Have a Dream," he looked forward to the time when freedom would finally ring from the Alleghenies to Stone Mountain, Georgia, and the molehills of Mississippi, when black and white would hold hands and sing, "Free at last, free at last,/Thank God Almighty, we're free at last!" Moved by this vision, he strode toward that freedom. Dreamers like King caught the picture of the plight of the poor, the young, and the black, and gave leadership in the pilgrimage toward liberation and reconciliation.

Eschatological eyes ranging over the terrain of the '70s come to rest on a people too long unseen. As blacks were "invisible men," so "forgotten Americans" have also been overlooked. Visionaries of the '70s will catch sight of Archie Bunker as a desperate human being whose angers and hates are rooted in profound frustrations and needs. The decade requires a fresh wave of dreamers who will sketch pictures of a new world for middle Americans, one in which the mills where they work, the cities and suburbs in which they dwell, the hospitals in which they suffer, the government under which they live, the marketplaces in which they buy and sell are human places where justice is done and peace is made; where the air they breathe, the food they eat, and the water they drink are safe and sound; and even where the "Archies" and the "Meatheads" will beat their swords into plowshares.

To look at the life of a middle American in this decade in the light of the biblical dream of shalom is to be shocked into an awareness of that life's torn and tattered fabric. Two things stand out: bondage to the "principalities and powers," and the erosion of life and its quality.

Bondage: In the kingdom of God citizens are free. In the world of the '70s, middle Americans are subject to the whims of technocratic processes and powers that hurl them into unemployment (both the Pittsburgh steelworker and the Boston Route 128 engineer), send their sons off to a cruel and inane war, manipulate their psyches in advertising and entertainment, peer into their privacy by sophisticated methods of surveillance, treat them as a button number at the mill gate, a card in an IBM machine, a vote on a precinct list, or "the ulcer in 307" of the mass medical center. "They" is a familiar word in the lexicon of blue- and white-collar workers who feel their lives are controlled by some distant Kafka-like castle.

Erosion: The principalities and powers that arrange the destinies of middle Americans are not known for their benign intentions or performance. By omission or commission they are responsible for that assortment of irritations and debilitations that has come to be the daily fare for Archie and his kin. While he lives above the poverty line (except when the periodic bottoming of a boom-and-bust economy puts him on unemployment insurance or the welfare rolls), that existence just inside the margins of security subjects him to a new set of erosive forces. The plastic world of consumer products available to lower-middle-income groups increasingly turns out to be the "ticky-tacky" house, toy, tool, clothing, and car. Programmed by the advertiser to believe that the bright and shiny new product is a little piece of paradise, the middle American soon enough finds his dream vanishing in breakage and shrinkage. And along with the decay there is serious danger. The risk of driving in eggshell autos eventuates in a highway death toll that has during the ten Vietnam war years added up to ten times the number of Americans killed on the battlefield. Must the penalty of both guilty and innocent driver and passenger be a form of capital punishment? Not to mention the increasingly predictable need to recall millions of unsafe vehicles bought by unsuspecting citizens. The quickening momentum of Ralph Nader and the consumer movement is a symptom of the populist determination to challenge the principalities and powers responsible for these outrages.

Eroding goods are matched by corroding services. Documentaries and studies exposing the inadequacy of hospital, medical, and dental care are becoming commonplace. The state of the public schools is in question. The cost and quality of funeral service are under scrutiny. The treatment and housing of the mentally ill and the aged step into the light of public examination and reproof. In these areas, as in the purchase of products, the middle American is the principal consumer, and therefore pays the heaviest cost in life and its quality.

The new ecological sensitivity has revealed the toll taken by a deteriorating environment on middle America. Blue-collar workers in mill town, small city, and large urban areas breathe, and have their lives shortened by, air fouled by the very furnaces they stoke. Mill workers will tell you, as they told me for ten years in a Pittsburgh steel-town ministry as I visited the hospitals and buried the dead, that the Donora-like air does mean work for them. So they put up with it. There is a difficult problem here of sorting out priorities, taking into account both economic need and technological ravage. While there are yet no absolutely clear guidelines, it is indisputable that the industrial poison in the air, water, and soil does serious harm to those who live and work in proximity to it—middle Americans.

On top of the contest with industrial impuri-
ties, there is the matter of psychic and even
physical survival in the urban (and suburban)
habitat, given the hours spent daily in traffic
hassles, the breakdown of public transportation,
filth, crime hazards, the meaninglessness of the
very jobs they covet, and the general normless-
ness of life in a modern megalopolis. It is little
wonder that Archie comes home angry every
day, grabs his can of Schlitz, sinks into his
overstuffed chair, turns on the TV, and turns off
the world.

Archie Bunker's attempt to shut out disso-
nance, turn back the clock, and put down the
dissenter are intimately related to his own mis-
eries. Visionaries who can see past his lances will
find there a wounded human being. And in his
wife Edith they will see no "dingbat," but a
human face.

It is hopeful to note some growing evidences
of this eschatological eyesight in the Christian
community. It is to be found in ethnic sectors of
middle America, and particularly among Roman
Catholics sensitive to their own constituencies
(in ways similar to the leadership given by black
churchmen to their people in an earlier decade).
Monsignor Geno Baroni of the National Conference on Urban Ethnic Affairs is a significant
practitioner of this newly sighted Christianity.[4]

[4] See Geno Baroni, ed., *All Men Are Brothers* (Washington,
D.C.: Task Force on Urban Problems, United States Catholic
Conference, 1970).

Michael Novak and Andrew Greeley have made astute cultural and theological analyses of their people's condition.[5] And in the Jewish community the American Jewish Committee and Murray Friedman demonstrated an early prophetic awareness of middle America.[6] Protestantism, whose pews are filled with middle Americans, not the least being Archie and Edith Bunker, has yet to develop comparable clarity of vision. But those committed to the End of the Story and its anticipation in the chapter on Incarnation must someday see that even the Bunkers are "all in the family" of God.

Storytellers have something to say about Now realities as well as Not Yet visions. It is because they have dreamed dreams that they can perceive the realities. Their view through the aperture of Jesus Christ into the shalom God intends for his world makes them conscious of the forces inimical to it. The fundamental factor that materializes under the searchlight of shalom is human perversity. Visionaries discover that lethal factor first in themselves as they measure their lives against the kingdom and its King. Finding this self-aggrandizing impulse down deep in their center, they are not taken aback by

---

[5] Michael Novak, *The Rise of the Unmeltable Ethnics* (New York: Macmillan, 1972), and Andrew Greeley, *Why Can't They Be Like Us?* (New York: Dutton, 1971).

[6] Murray Friedman, ed., *Overcoming Middle-Class Rage* (Philadelphia: Westminster, 1971); Judith Magidson, *Reacting Americans* (The American Jewish Committee, 1968).

its omnipresence in the world. The same Christian realism observes that the temptation to escalate the "I, me, and mine" advances with the growth of power over others. Visionary realists are driven by the discovery of these facts to the other side of the Cross. The suffering and death of Jesus is not only a gleam to follow but also a gift to receive. It draws from them a penitence that acknowledges complicity in the crucifixion of shalom, a trust in an incredible Mercy yet willing to cover that guilt, and a sober realization of the continuing presence of self-regarding and other-ignoring inclinations. To the enigmas of Archie Bunker they bring their experience and understanding of guilt and grace.

An eye for reality will, of course, see the obvious—Archie Bunker is a sinner too. He is preoccupied with his comfort and conveniences, hardened to the plight of the poor and the black, captive to all kinds of chauvinist demons. On top of the manifest "shutupness" (Kierkegaard) of his ways, he is also party to the very crimes of the society from which he suffers. By sins of omission he allows the powers that be to run roughshod over him. And by lethargy and shortsightedness he contributes to the wastes and wanderings of the time. The twin culpabilities of human nature—pride and lassitude, arrogance and copping out—are there for realistic eyes to see.

A simple moralism will be content to scold Archie. Its sister mentality, an individualistic pietism, will do the same, adding to it the promise of total cure if he hits the sawdust trail. A visionary realism has another kind of perception. While never relaxing the mandates of divine obedience directed toward middle America, and always keeping alive the Word of forgiveness, it knows about the persistence and depth of egoism, even among the "converted" on whom the pietist pins his hopes. Its understanding of redemption includes asking the question: How can the self-regarding givens, which will be with us until God brings in his kingdom, be harnessed to the very purposes of that vision? Can the "self-interest" that ranges all the way from the will to survive the daily rat race to "getting mine" be channeled into strategies that might point themselves to liberation and reconciliation?

This kind of visionary realism has affinities with the "practical idealism" of a Saul Alinsky who worked for changing society not by "appealing to the better nature" of either oppressor or oppressed, but by forceful attention to the complaints and wants of little people. It is significant that several years before he died Alinsky declared the next major front line for humanizing our society to be middle America, and began to direct his organizational skills to that end.[7] He believed that for two reasons. One is related to the point we are presently exam-

[7] Saul Alinsky, *Rules for Radicals* (New York: Random, 1970), pp. 185ff.

ining—middle Americans are in trouble and are
beginning to clamor for recognition and rights.
The second has to do with the power they
represent, another learning from realism to
which we shall presently turn.

A kindred grasp of reality is the "consciousness-raising" program of movements for wom-
en's liberation. Attention is focused by the aggrieved on injustices suffered and identities submerged. Neither an Alinsky with his brand of
community organization nor women's groups
who are intensifying awarenesses of trampled
rights believe that having and sharing visions is
enough to change things for the better. Thus
realism rejects moral exhortation as the simple
key to social change. Whether these same movements have sufficient openness to the pain and
pressure of the vision of reconciliation stew-
arded by moralists, along with the thrust toward
liberation, is a question visionary realists must
put to these and other realists.

The implication of this understanding of reality is the need to raise the middle-American
consciousness of personal hurt and hope. "You
people are 'niggers' too," said a minority-group
militant to an assembly of well-intentioned
middle-class churchmen. "Until you realize that
and make common cause with us, neither of us
is going to get anywhere."[8] Self-discovery of the
nature and sources of modern dehumanization

[8] A Chicano priest addressing the COCU assembly in Denver,
1971.

reveals the abyss shared by both the vocal
minority and the "silent majority." The recognition of a common self-interest, and the possibility of joining forces to deal with it, is the way
the pit walls are negotiated.[9] The realism of the
Christian Story as it touches this arena of human
life sensitizes hurt people and their allies to their
own plight.

To what end? In partnership with raising the
threshold of awareness goes the recognition that
the sources of oppression are also moved by
their interests, in this case large, vested ones.
Compounding the self-regard, here, is its massive
power. Fed by the growth of that power toward
monolithic proportions, the self-regard becomes
more lethal. The centers of economic, political,
and social power, with their attendant elites, will
not relinquish their hold on the instruments of
self-aggrandizement because visionaries paint
pictures of how things should be. The principalities and powers need to be challenged and
balanced by other centers of power, with all
pyramidal decision-making finally dispersed and
democratized.[10] Middle Americans must gener-
ate their own countervailing social, economic,
and political influences. Consciousness-raising is
done, therefore, in order to organize centers of
power that will call to account the erosive forces
playing upon the lives and fortunes of middle

[9] For a discussion of the pit image as a clue to social change,
see *Liberation in Middle America, op. cit.*, pp. 70-78.
[10] A point driven home with regularity by Reinhold Niebuhr.

Americans. Where the understanding of the wiles of human sin is fully grasped, there will be no illusions about the effects of any new power so acquired by middle Americans. They are subject to the same temptations and corruptions. Such sobriety will build into the middle-American quest for countervailing strengths its own set of internal checks and balances.

The same realism that presses Archie Bunker to organize pushes him yet further to new relationships with old enemies. To fulfill his goals, to muster sufficient social power to humanize his life in the realms of consumption, work, play, environment, urban habitat, war, and peace, he is forced to look for allies who are also suffering and struggling for their own dignity. Ironically, the unyoung, the unpoor, and the unblack must turn to the young, the poor, and the black whom they so recently made the target of their ire (during a Babylonian captivity in which the principalities and powers played the game of divide and conquer, encouraging the suicidal infighting of potential allies). Through the back door elements of the Christian vision come into range of this realism, for new efforts at reconciliation are vital to the coalitions necessitated by the quest for sufficient countervailing power.

But visions must be more than inadvertent and covert in Storytellers. Their gentle pressure has to be felt in any faithful application of the Tale to the times. Thus for the visionary realist there can be no uncritical talk of the push and pull of power. Efforts at social change must begin at "zero alienation," although they may not be able to end there if tyranny continues unabated. But the Cross *is* the place where divine power chose powerlessness. The exercise of raw power with its Machiavellian twists and turns is not an option for those who live at the juncture of vision and reality. While the purity of the vision of cheek-turning shalom cannot be exported neatly from the end of history into the middle of it—a corrupt world regularly crucifies its Christ-figures and slaughters its innocents— the vision can modify, judge, and keep off balance any strategies that threaten to mistake provisional wielding of power with the way of the kingdom of God. For those lured by a longer Future in which leopard and kid lie down together, there is sober recognition that all necessary exercises in power fall short of the standard and goal of shalom. And with it, there is a profoundly personal anguish that people "on the other side of the barricades" are being hurt and Christ is again being crucified. Such a penitence drives the believer back again and again to a Cross that is alone able to cope with the guilt that comes from the wounding of God. Action and evangel will meet regularly on the battlefield of middle America.

By using the motifs of vision and reality we have tried to show how the Christian drama finds its way into our own day-to-day life. As much as

it sheds light on the problems, it also is illumined by rays reflected from them. And its
personal address to us comes forcefully home
when we hear it from within the historical arena
itself.

As engagement evangelism explores the Christian Story's bearing on matters of culture, the
shape of that Story itself comes clear through
the looking glass of culture. And in that same
mirror we may be able to see also who we are,
where we are going, and what we must do.

## CHAPTER SIX

# Going East:
# Neomysticism
# and Christian Faith

While bombs were being planted in campus research centers in the fall of 1970, University of Hawaii students witnessed another kind of confrontation. A graffiti war was in progress at a central construction site. One week the fences read, "Come Sunday night to 1212 University Avenue. Psychic sleep, natural high. Hare Krishna, Hare Krishna, Krishna Krishna, Hare Hare, Hare Rama. . . ." The next week the mantras disappeared and in their place appeared, "Jesus loves you. Flee hell, find heaven. Turn on with Christ, 20th and Pahoa Ave., 7:15 P.M., Mondays." Moreover, the attacking "Jesus freaks" announced they were going to carry the battle to the streets of Waikiki. There, in front of the International Market Place, the chanting Krishnites would be lovingly enveloped by the sounds and sights of "Onward Christian Soldiers."

How do these religious impulses relate to the Christian Story, and how does the Christian community relate to them? The new mysticism abroad among the young poses fundamental questions to an engaged evangelism.

## Technocracy's Rebels

Whether they read it in the pages of Theodore Roszak's *The Making of a Counter Culture* or Charles Reich's *The Greening of America*, or come to it as the result of a hassle at a peace demonstration, a pot party bust, or involvement in an ecological crusade, there is a common picture in the head developing among the arriving generation of middle-class young. They look out on a society framed by its picture tubes, high rises, and jet vapor trails. In that scene all the modern techniques from lasers to miniature circuitry conspire to revolutionize the worlds of work and play. Back of the products lie the premises: the methods of the laboratory and the shop floor—empirical, rational, pragmatic— define the limits of reality, prescribe the right way to deal with it, and promise a horn of plenty. Further, way up there somewhere at the controls of these awesome instruments seem to be cadres of "experts" with their own plans and plots. Sometimes this high scheming appears to be done in such compartmentalized fashion that it looks like "nobody is in charge."

And what have these gods wrought? Plague,

pestilence, famine, and death. The divine promises of technocracy have not been kept; instead
of fulfillment has come the apocalypse of pollu-
tion, hunger, hate, and war.

If the science-technology of the West has
brought us to a dead end, then it's time to look
for another way out, so the scenario reads. Go
East, young human. Those who tread this new
path will not tinker with the outer world but
will discover and relate to the inner cosmos; not
seek to subdue and control everything but
groove with the All; not reason and dissect, but
experience and feel; not talk, talk, talk, nor act,
act, act, but meditate and contemplate; not revel
in things man-made and urban, but learn to love
things natural and close to the soil; not be at-
tracted to the complexity, hardness, and pre-
cision of the technician, but to the simplicity,
softness, and gentleness of the guru; not live by
the creed that it's every man for himself and the
devil take the hindmost, but believe in human
goodness, risk the act of sharing, and affirm
things communal; not adopt the rigid manners
and morals of middle America, but be "freed
up" in life-style from hair and clothing to music
and mating. The birth of the "new religions"
(the title of Jacob Needleman's work on neomysticism) of feeling, fantasy, mystery, and
communality is a natural expression of the new
quest.

One other stream feeding into the romantic
reaction to technocracy and its failures, rein-

forcing particularly the mystical aspects, is the
personal struggle to assess the relation of chem-
ical stimulation of the brain to our perception of
reality. Sometimes psychedelic drugs are used in
conjunction with religious rituals. More often,
devotees declare that they no longer require
artificial stimuli since a "natural high" is available to them through their new-found rites. The
attempt to grasp and manipulate the physiologi-
cal routes of enlightenment has recently led to
the invention of the alphaphone, a technological
device that facilitates the production of brain
waves associated with some kinds of religious
experience. Oh final irony! In any case, a certain
love-hate relationship with a chemistry that
promises better things for better living contributes to the neomystical fevers.

## Another East

What is the church's response to the neomystic? It begins with real human relationships
by churchmen with these constituencies, and
support for their communities when under
harassment. But it goes on from that to probing
and sharing. We focus initially on the varieties of
"Eastern religion" that dominate the current
religious scene ("Christ is dead—Buddha lives!"
is the subtitle of John Garabedian and Orde
Coombs' study of this phenomenon, *Eastern
Religions in the Electric Age).* [1]

[1] See John Garabedian and Orde Coombs, *Eastern Religions
in the Electric Age* (New York: Grosset and Dunlap, 1969);

Worth mentioning is a rather obvious but almost universally ignored fact: Christianity is also an Eastern religion. So is Judaism. As such, they are sensitive to the dimensions of mystery and unity that draw the counter-culture to other Eastern options. Eastern Orthodox explore hidden depths of the spirit, St. Francis celebrates the living earth of the ecologists, and communitarian experiments abound in Christian history. Counterparts to all are found in Judaism. The Western Christianity in which these perceptions are buried has so accommodated to its technocratic setting that it is difficult for the young to see these riches. But they are there.

However, they are there with a difference. The spirituality growing out of the Judeo-Christian stream practices a contemplation that is companion to action and talk, rather than polarized with them. The Presence is sought in the midst of social and political ferment, not in flight from them. In our own times, those seeking that Presence set their faces against the same technocracy and rationalism rejected by the counter-culture, but refuse to accept the anti-technological and anti-intellectual mold in which the neomystic protest is cast.

The diverging styles are traceable to a fundamental difference in source: one oriental religious tradition broke step with its sisters. Jews and Christians do not move toward, nor are they

Richard Woods, *The Occult Revolution* (New York: Herder and Herder, 1971); and Jacob Needleman, *The New Religions* (Garden City, N. Y.: Doubleday, 1970).

moved by, what Arend Th. van Leeuwen calls
the "basic apperception" that underlies their
Eastern kin, an intuition that he believes may be
dormant in all of us.[2] This intuition is of the
essential unity of all things, which is more fundamental than the diversities and alienations
that daily assault us. Religions that cultivate this
apprehension testify to the illusoriness of the
self and the passingness of history, seek to slow
time down for unseeking contemplation of "the
abiding present" (Alan Watts), and strive for
fusion with the All. Cultural fruits of this orientation include the encouragement of what van
Leeuwen calls the "ontocratic pattern," the for-
mation of political hierarchies and caste structures that have the stamp of approval of the
cosmos itself. The new Aquarians lodge their
protest against technocracy, and express their
longing for unity, in this kind of religious sensi-
bility. And their apolitical life-style leaves un-
challenged the castes and hierarchies created by
the gods of our own secular society.

It is tempting to speculate about the relation
of Aquarian drug experience (immersion in "the
private sea") to the religious trip that invites
absorption of the droplet of self in the sea of
Reality (see Thomas Braden's *The Private Sea*
and *The Age of Aquarius*),[3] and in turn to the

---

[2] Arend Th. van Leeuwen, *Christianity in World History*,
trans. H. H. Hoskins (New York: Scribner's, 1964).

[3] Thomas Braden, *The Age of Aquarius* (Chicago: Quadrangle,
1970) and *The Private Sea: LSD and the Search for God*
(Chicago: Quadrangle, 1967).

"fundamental apperception." Do the former "develop" the last as a film in solution? Do Freud's comments on religion as "oceanic feeling" add any light to the connections? We leave such questions open-ended, being concerned here to suggest how neomysticism may be part of a wider religious phenomenon that takes its cues from a direction very different from that of one small, stubborn Near Eastern tribe.

The singularity of Israel lay in its own orientation point for mystery and unity: not in and down, but out and ahead. It took its bearings from events in its history and saw these happenings as disclosures of a *promised* Reality. It was not mesmerized by a stationary Light shining from the depths, but kept its eye upon a pillar of fire up front that lured its people out of the past, through the present, toward a Not Yet. The Christian community took up this future-oriented covenant, seeing Bethlehem, Galilee, Golgotha, Easter, and Pentecost in continuity with Exodus. And the New Israel believed, and believes, that the rays of the ever receding horizon Light have been caught in the mirror of these Jesus events.

What one does in the light of this lure of futurity is very different from the neomystic who seeks to penetrate the veil of the temporal Now by an interior descent into the divine effulgence. On the one hand, there is an abiding curiosity about certain past happenings because these events are knotholes into the future. And there is a zeal to tell and celebrate the revelatory tales. On the other hand, the vision of how the world could be, and will be, is so different from the way it is now that the visionary cannot be servile before the givens, inner or outer. He is goaded to rearrange and bend them into signposts toward the future.

Let us focus in more closely on two aspects of the Story's final chapter: relationships to nature and history. In doing it we shall look more particularly, also, at some of the characteristics of the biblical vision.

Nature—The great dream of fulfillment is, as we have said, one of shalom. The soil and the sea, the plants and the animals, are all part of that final hope for wholeness, unity, peace. Rich biblical metaphors point to the healing of a crippled creation: the wolf and the lamb together, the child able to put her hand over the asp's hole, the fields fertile, the groaning creation singing the songs of joy. The foretaste of, and mandate toward, that End are found in the one who stills the tempest and overcomes the final wound of physical things in his resurrection. Moreover, he furnishes us with a new pair of eyes to see in nature the healing rhythms already at work in the birds of the air and the flowers of the field, earnests of a coming shalom.

To one community within the realm of nature comes a special charge to build the earth toward that vision. Rooted in the natural world, yet gifted as well with a power to imagine and act upon fresh scenarios, the human race is called to co-responsibility with the Builder. The project is harassed on every side: with the fitful labor and absenteeism of the craftsmen; their inclination to throw up Babels whose weight fractures the earth and whose collapse scatters the work teams; the failures of the materials themselves, nature's own internal breakdowns. But creation and re-creation go on apace with signs of hope left by their Source in the works of nature and man.

That kind of perspective begets these kinds of affirmations and warnings: science-technology, as humanity's most recent expression of its capacity to understand the workings of its world and the freedom to ennoble it, becomes a potential ally in the call to build the earth. With the readiness to use this awesome instrument come some sobering sister commitments: (1) an awareness of the temptations to abuse power that parasite upon human ingenuity; (2) sensitivity to the delicate textures of healing that are already in nature, and in the company of which the work of building is to go on; and (3) loyalty to the final vision of shalom by which all the technological blueprints must be measured.

There is here no romanticism of nature nor invitation to melt into it. Nature is short of its goal and broken in the pursuit of it. But it is not evil or illusory. While not God, it is good, a piece of the final dream and a partner in the journey toward new creation. Humanity is to honor the traces of the future there, and be an active agent of their upbuilding.

History—The same action toward the future is to be found in our dealings with history. The new heavens and new earth house a New Jerusalem. This picture of a new society on the screen of tomorrow lures us away from the present and makes impossible any sacral confirmation of the way things are. There is no rigid social structure given approval by cosmic forces. Nor is there any guarantee of an Eternal Now that can be reached by passage through, or descent below, this "withoutness." Society's patterns are human, not divine, a product of that part of creation freed to make its own way toward a temporarily distanced Vision. The sacred is not a *fait accompli*, but a task to be done and a promise to be kept. Historical action is charged to call into question all structures that militate against that Not Yet, and build new ones that chase the dream.

While history is littered with shattered dreams, it is not one vast trash can. Contrary to simple-minded futurisms, the time before the End is not God-forsaken. The absolute future appears, not only in Christ, but, fleetingly, wherever glimmers of shalom are to be seen. This kind of nowness is the ground of hope. But more, it gives direction to the inwardness appropriate to future-oriented faith. Devotion is through a glass darkly, eschatologically modest, communion not union, sacramental not sacral.

And the sacramental happens, as did the first sacrament, in the moil and toil of things. All this is a long way from the mystical and neomystical quest for healing in the waters of the womb.

## The Jesus People

Where do the Jesus people fit in? They are both more and less than their professed identity.

The conventional fundamentalist who courts the young Jesus people may be in for a surprise. While their vocabulary resembles that of a very conservative Christianity, the timing of their appearance on the religious scene, their counter-culture garb and hair style, and sometimes their communal life-style hint that we have to do with something more than a restoration of "the old-time religion." Some of their identification tags suggest that they are part of the same revolt against the society of their elders as the self-consciously oriental varieties of religious experience. The Jesus people have seized upon more readily accessible symbols to express their Consciousness III sensibilities. (Is this strategically wiser than those who reach for the bizarre, or does it suggest a more domesticated rebellion? The signs point to the latter. While the Krishnites dominated the religious street scene in cosmopolitan Honolulu, the Jesus people were drawing hundreds of teen-agers to meetings in Kailua, a largely middle-class, white suburb.) What effect this will have on the conservative

Christianity that currently harbors them should make an interesting story.

From our angle of vision, the Jesus people are also, sadly, less than their Christian identity implies. To date there is little evidence of their commitment to an event-grounded and future-oriented faith. The new pietism nestles as comfortably into oppressive political and economic systems as any other neomysticism. Judging from the life-style of its proponents, turning on with Jesus means dropping out of the social struggle. A Christ so easily domesticated in the present and imprisoned in the soul is hardly recognizable. Neither is one who encourages uncritical acceptance of biblical literalism, religious fantasy, and the abdication of the intellectual quest. In both its strong and weak points, therefore—as a critic of technocracy, and offering alternatives to it—the "Jesus trip" appears to be more a creature of the counter-culture than an authentic recovery of the powerful symbols of the Christian faith.

The other popular Jesus cult, devotion associated with the rock opera *Superstar*, is also both more and less than its label might suggest. Along with the rest of the counter-culture, the music launches an attack on the sentimentalities of the Establishment, in this case particularly the conventional wisdom about an unworldly Jesus. When it rejects the "docetism" (neglect of the human and earthy) of conventional religion and underscores the humanity of Jesus, the opera is more orthodox than it realizes. In fact, it should shame all of us in the church for being so long party to the anemic caricature of an enfleshed God. But its rendition of Jesus as a superstar in the current anti-hero tradition is such an echo of going assumptions of Aquarians that the radical over-againstness of Jesus is censored and the Gospel thoroughly tamed. Like most of the biographies of Christ, *Superstar* is autobiography. As such it is incapable of doing the critical and revolutionary work a characterization of Christ must do to be faithful to the God who refuses to be made over in our image.

*Relationships of the Christian Community and the New Religions*

Out of this sorting and sifting come some guidelines for relating to neomysticism and neomystics.

(1) Behind and through the often strange religious idiom, profound human insights and astute social criticism are to be found. Neomysticism exposes gaping holes in our society. Its rituals and fantasies are cries from those wounded by technocratic machinery (neomystics and middle Americans have more in common than is often realized). On the other hand, its reveries and disciplines point to how the world could be if another cultural course were to be taken. The communitarian experiments undertaken in the light of the new visions should

disturb us and call us toward new social forms and life-styles. Beyond being symptoms and signs, new religious patterns may also be ways of coping. Why should not "yoga over forty" lead to new self-understanding and health for middle-aged Christians? Further, human tenderness and ecological sensitivity are in short supply in a technocratic era, and are to be applauded for what they are even when in exotic garb. Again, contemplation and meditation are valuable ways of centering down in our chaotic and harried daily routines. These are all secular insights into the ways of healing and dream of wholeness. Let us, then, secularize them. Honor them for their value by detaching them from the religious paraphernalia and using them in the service of shalom.

(2) In neomysticism there are more specifically religious, as well as ethical, resonances of the Christian faith. The refusal to accept things seen as final reality is surely one of them. The love of God for his own sake is another. The pressures of a pragmatic and secular time have tried mightily to program out these intimations of transcendence. We can be grateful to the protestations of the neomystic for making us more alert to this captivity. Perhaps we must do some much more serious digging in our own mystical traditions—from the Eastern churches to the Western mystics—for these latter gropings build their window into Reality with the action- and future-oriented tools of the biblical tradition.

(3) The popular slogan of the '60s calling for a "moratorium on God-talk" ought to be re-examined. The neomystical stirrings are one more reason why we must recover the Story-telling dimension of the church's mission. For humans whose wounds are not only physical, and whose thirst is for mystery and meaning, other options from the East must find their place alongside those of the swami and guru.

## CHAPTER SEVEN

# The Story and the Parish

Many current Jesus devotees—from fans of Superstar to "street people"—have little use for organized religion. Sweeping new enthusiasms are frequently anti-institutional. However, Christ is no disembodied spirit. He is the Head of a Body. The church, where the Story is regularly told, celebrated, and done, is the Body of Christ. With all its failings, it is still the object of divine care. God is used to loving the unlovable *(agape)*. If the church is good enough for him, we are ill-advised to circumvent it.

Underscoring this theological truth are some sociological facts of life. Somewhere there has to be a careful institutional effort to steward the fulness of a mission so vulnerable to constant fragmentation. That leads us right to the most pervasive expression of the church, the parish. Can the local church be that good steward of the wholeness of the Body?

A decade ago many were agitated by the

question, "Is the local church obsolete?"[1]
Critics doubted that the parish could minister to
a mobile, secular population, address its power
structures, or deal responsibly with the ethical
dilemmas of modern society from its residential
base.[2] Prophetic voices also lashed out at the
complacency of the membership. Alternative
structures—para-parochial and supra-parochial—
were launched. An era of coffeehouses, industrial missions, leisure ministries, house churches,
task forces, and movements for social change
gained momentum. This brilliant array of experimentation has dimmed. A faltering economy
took its toll on church budgets, which in turn
viewed innovation as an expendable item. Polari-
zation contributed to the financial cutbacks, for
new ministries were often thought of as anti-
establishment, as were their national funding
agencies. Innovators too frequently fueled these
fires by their adventurism.

[1] For a review of the main themes of that criticism and its
literature see the author's "The Crisis of the Congregation: A
Debate," in *Voluntary Associations*, ed. D. B. Robertson (Rich-
mond, Va.: Knox, 1966), pp. 275-279.

[2] As in such popular critiques as Gibson Winter's *The Subur-
ban Captivity of the Church* (New York: Macmillan, 1962) and
*The New Creation as Metropolis* (New York: Macmillan, 1963);
Peter Berger's *The Noise of Solemn Assemblies* (Garden City,
N.Y.: Doubleday, 1961); and Colin Williams' *Where in the
World?* (New York: National Council of Churches, 1963) and
*What in the World?* (New York: National Council of Churches,
1964). The debate unfolded in the "Missionary Structure Study"
of the World Council of Churches, and can be traced in detail in
the issues of *Concept* (blue and red issues), from 1962 to 1970.

While some significant efforts are still with us,[3] as is the evidence that the local church is *not* omnicompetent and desperately needs extra-parochial allies,[4] the fact is that the parish endures as our fundamental base of operations. It is "hic et nunc," here and now, as one of the earliest of the era's church renewers, Abbé Michonneau, tried to remind those who expected its early demise and replacement by an assortment of new forms. Added to this is the coming into its own of Story-telling, the function of the local church that even its sharpest critics affirmed.[5] And now even the conventional wisdom of the '60s—"we do not live where we live"—that the residential community is a marginal phenomenon, is being challenged by a new spate of commentary on the importance of things local and "the integrity of place."[6] Thus we return to the grass-roots life of the congregation to ask how this people of God can be faithful to the full orb of nurture and mission.

The pluralism of purpose and cross-pollina-

[3] See Joan Thatcher, *The Church Responds* (Valley Forge, Pa.: Judson, 1970).

[4] The alliance between the local church and extra-parochial forms is discussed in *The Pastor and the World* (Philadelphia: United Church, 1964), pp. 39-64.

[5] Peter Berger, "Letter on the Parish Ministry," *The Christian Century*, Vol. LXXXI, No. 18 (April 29, 1964), pp. 549f.

[6] For example, Peter Schrag, *The Decline of the WASP* (New York: Simon and Schuster, 1971); Michael Novak, *The Rise of the Unmeltable Ethnics, op. cit.*; and Martin Marty, *Context* (published by the Thomas More Association), July 1, 1972, *passim*.

tion affirmed throughout our inquiry must take form in the congregation. In examining how this might be done, we refine further the manifoldness of mission discussed in Chapter 1 by taking some cues from the language and accents of the earliest Christians. Its congregations faced the same question of blending the one and the many, especially so the church at Corinth (I Cor. 12-14). We lift out four themes that recur in the first decades of Christianity: *kerygma, diakonia, koinonia,* and *leitourgia*—telling, doing, being, celebrating. The church strives toward fulness when it is engaged in all: proclamation, service, fellowship, and worship.

The New Testament communities that carried on these activities were all aimed outward. They did not exist, first and foremost, for themselves, but constituted a "church for others." Each of the four themes was pointed in the direction of the world: Christians were determined to preach the Gospel to the "uttermost parts of the earth" and "to the end of the age." They carried on their ministry of healing and serving for the stranger and the neighbor; they lived out their life together as a candle on a candlestand, prompting the testimony, "See how these Christians love one another"; their first public celebration at Pentecost was a missionary worship. The movement outward is grounded in the very self-emptying of God in the person and work of Jesus Christ, the "mission of God" that finds its response in our mission to the world.

While mission is the defining characteristic of

the church, it is also true that the congregations
carried on within their own life a counterpart to
each of these four outward-jutting prongs.
*Nurture* was the partner of, and training ground
for, *mission*. An intramural *telling* went on in
preaching, teaching, and sharing of faith within
the community. *Doing* was directed to the
orphans, widows, slaves, and poor of the congregation in addition to the stranger. *Being* together
was an act of the catacombs as well as the
marketplace. And *celebrating* was not only
public (liturgy of the catechumens), but also
intimate (liturgy of the faithful).

A structure for congregational life today that
learns from the double expression of the four
dimensions of faith would look like this:

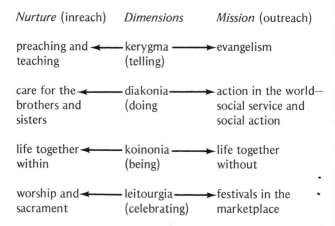

| *Nurture* (inreach) | *Dimensions* | *Mission* (outreach) |
|---|---|---|
| preaching and ◄──── kerygma ────► evangelism<br>teaching                  (telling) | | |
| care for the ◄──── diakonia ────► action in the world—<br>brothers and        (doing              social service and<br>sisters                                      social action | | |
| life together ◄──── koinonia ────► life together<br>within                    (being)              without | | |
| worship and ◄──── leitourgia ────► festivals in the<br>sacrament            (celebrating)      marketplace | | |

A whole Body of Christ will include all these
parts. A local congregation committed to the

fulness of nurture and mission will constantly be asking itself: "Have we got it all together?" Is each dimension being honored in both its inreach and its outreach? And is there a joining and working together of parts as befits a living Body?

The wholeness and variety appropriate to the Body of Christ force us to ask whether a single congregation has the resources for such stewardship. In ancient usage, a "heresy" is a partial truth inflated to appear as the full Gospel. Today, one of our most dangerous heresies may be ecclesiastical institutions that carry out parts of the church's purpose but ignore others. Local congregations sensitive to the fragmentary nature of their own ministry will explore the possibilities of partnership with other congregations and institutions. Let us examine one model that looks toward the breaking down of the dividing walls among congregations at the local level for the sake of the wholeness of the Body and the fulness of the Gospel. While it might be used by a single church with unusual resources, it is designed for open congregations moving toward cluster with others, or beyond such cooperation to even larger ecumenical visions.[7]

## Unity and Pluralism at the Grass Roots

Some years ago Stephen Rose offered a pro-

[7] For the relation of the three motifs to a wider ecumenism see Gabriel Fackre, "Parsimony, Pluralism, and the COCU Parish," in *Church Union at Mid-Point* (New York: Association, 1972), ed. William Boney.

posal for local ministry with three bases of operation.[8] His prescience about the need for pluralism has been borne out. However, some fresh things have come clear regarding the nature, direction, and interaction of the component parts. We therefore begin with a three-pronged conception of local church life, interpreting and refining it in the light of our earlier discussion.

The imperatives of telling the Story point toward a kerygmatic center where this dimension is accorded its full importance. Here serious and sustained attention is given to the fundamental symbols and meanings of the Christian faith. And this in its two directions, inreach and outreach. Within the center the young and newly received are introduced to the Story. Those already acquainted with it are trained to grow in their understanding. In tandem with this nurture is the work of evangelism, the going out of the Word. The thrust beyond might include the conclave ministries discussed earlier as well as other outreach (with the enclave on the boundary between nurture and evangelism). Kerygmatic communication need not be housed in the building designated for these concerns, but can occur also in satellite activity. The "telling center" would draw to itself a group of people whose gifts and interests could find their focus in nurture and evangelism.

From a companion location, with its accompanying constituency, rise the service ministries. Out from here extends the reach toward society's victims. The "doing center" would address itself to the issues of poverty, race, war, environment, the rights of minorities, and other current issues of humanization. It would express itself in "social service"—the binding up of wounds—and "social action"—dealing with the forces and structures that inflict them. Along with this outreach, this center would attend to the needs of members of the congregation, ranging from counseling and visitation to job assistance and services to the elderly. Just as the early church recognized the importance of a diaconate to take responsibility for its worldly matters, so the servanthood center enables the church to exercise its desperately needed secular ministry.

At a third location, a celebration center, is found the symbol of common life, "common worship." Here all the people gather periodically to affirm their unity with God and each other in Great Thanksgivings. In worship they declare that the small-center communities in which they regularly participate are eyes or hands that need the presence and interconnection of other parts in order to make up the Body.

The great celebrations might be weekly, or monthly, or at festival seasons. Alongside them there must be opportunity for the liturgical pluralism of the church to be honored. Here in the center worship styles might be provided that

range from Quaker silence, through high cere-
monial drama and straightforward preaching
services, to folk music and glossolalia gatherings.
But they all happen under the umbrella of the
parish, one large-visioned enough not to exclude
the least of these. At this center too there is the
planning and executing of celebrations beyond
the walls, running from banner marches to
marketplace festivals. For the enabling of worship there is a corps of celebrants.

As this center serves as the visible sign of the
unity of the parish, and facilitator of that unity,
other activities take place here, which might
better identify this base as "the center for celebration and coordination." The overall plotting
of the course of parish life is carried on here.
Times of cross-fertilization and mutual ministry
such as the congregational meeting and its planning task forces take place in it. Unity is given
some of its clearest credibility in actions that
celebrate common bonds such as baptism and
confirmation. In these acts, new covenants are
made with a God of all the people, and church
membership established as being membership in
all "the people of God in this place," the parish.

In many ways, the center for celebration and
coordination is the real test of the model. It is
clear from the experience of the past two eras of
church life discussed in Chapter 1, and from
experimentation with "house churches," that
the shared life together around a passionate
commitment makes for intense comradeship.

The centers will cultivate just that kind of "we group" feeling. This is particularly true today when a depersonalized society creates a thirst for intimacy and the need for "support systems." With the benefits of close community go the dangers of spiritual hauteur and separatism. Such a sect mentality draws a smaller and smaller circle of "true believers," and breeds a self-righteous fury that shatters the bond of a larger covenant. To discourage, or at the very least to mitigate, the pharisaism and split-off tendency that parasites upon highly charged group life, church membership is vested in the whole and not the part, in the parish not the conventicles of action, study, or prayer. Such a joining also means mutual accountability. The doers must report to, and hear out, the pray-ers, and vice versa. The tellers must relate to both.

Commingling, of course, happens outside the house of worship and planning. As we have sought to demonstrate throughout this study, telling cannot even be what it most essentially is unless it is carried on in the context of engagement with human issues. And doing and celebrating in Christian idiom are less than what they fundamentally are when disengaged from being and telling. Therefore within the very center for particularities, there is already built friendship with the accents of other centers, and a demand for alliance and interpenetration.

The coordinating center of the parish bears a special responsibility for seeing that cross-

pollination is a reality. As such it becomes a
protector of the theological credibility of the
congregation, a guarantee that sectarian fragmentation, and with it the half-truth, will be
discouraged.

There are centers for three of the four dimensions of the church. Where, then, is the vehicle
for koinonia in this pattern? There is no separate
site for koinonia, for each center individually
and corporately is called to be a home of
mutuality. Koinonia is a quality of life born in
the midst of the kerygmatic, diakonial, and
liturgical functions of the community. It comes
both in the deep sharings that happen in the
work of the centers and at the moments of
mutual ministry among them. Serving, teaching,
and worshipping can be designed. Life together
is an elusive wind that blows where it will.
Kerygma, diakonia, and leitourgia need their
tools and times. Koinonia can do with anything,
be with anyone, happen anytime. For the fourth
dimension there is no "place." We pray for the
grace of life together, to "let it be."

## A Note on Resources

A three-foci parish suggests a new design for
clergy. Beyond the jack-of-all-trades generalist,
on the one hand, and random staff specialist on
the other, there is the possibility of a division of
roles commensurate with the work of kerygma,
diakonia, and leitourgia. Each "pastor" would
relate to a constituency, and together they

would form a team that served the entire parish.

This model of ministry affords an opportunity to rejuvenate in a fresh way the ancient
threefold office (itself originally born of similar
demands). Thus the presbyter (priest) was called
to steward the mysteries of faith, the diaconate
created to carry out horizontal service ministries,
and the bishop appeared as the overseer of the
community and its great celebrations.

The old can reappear in our model with new
styles and accents. Ascendancy-submission patterns of former times, in the relations of clergy
to laity and to each other, are replaced by col-
legiality and alongsidedness. Rather than pre-
siding over the laity, they are "servants of the
servants of God," resources not sources. In the
place of a hierarchical arrangement that places
bishop, priest, and deacon in descending order,
there is partnership and co-equality within the
team, with special coordinating tasks ("under-
seeing," not overseeing) vested in the coordina-
tor. Thus for the telling center we have the
kerygmatic presbyter, for the doing center the
deacon, and for the worship center the cele-
brator-coordinator.

The functional model of parish life is a laboratory for all the themes we have been exploring
in this book. On the one hand, it must embody
the integrity of each facet of the faith community. In particular, the tandem centers of
evangel and action exist to honor and legitimate
the mandates of telling and doing. By situating
each in the institutional life of Christianity they

will not easily be uprooted by changing winds of doctrine. By providing a special orbit for those with kindred gift and spirit, there is a "getting it together" similar to the struggle for place and identity by minority groups imperiled by the absorptionist tendencies of the larger society. As black pride and cohesion establish identity, centers for "telling pride" and "doing pride" also provide strength. Each is a kind of "liberation movement" guaranteeing freedom of word and deed.

On the other hand, there must be a radical open-endedness and cross-fertilization of doing and telling constituencies and accents. As we have sought to show, any recounting of the Story faithful to its meaning will happen in the theater of sensitive action and actors. And, in turn, no action devoid of faith can be authentic Christian servanthood. As in movements for social change, so too here in the work of the Word, reconciliation is the crown and completion of liberation.

\*     \*     \*     \*     \*

To honor the parts yet affirm the whole—that is the difficult task of unity and diversity to which the Body of Christ in the '70s is called. Can the mainstream churches bring an orphaned telling back into the family, reacquainting her with her three sisters—doing, being, and celebrating? From such a reunion, born of the Holy Spirit, will come "a life with God in a church for the world."